WATER
IDEAS FOR LIFE

SURESH MADAMPIL

INDIA • SINGAPORE • MALAYSIA

"yapo divya uta va sravanti khanitrima uta va yah svayanjah

Samudrartha yah sucayah pavakas ta apo deviriha mamavantu"

"Waters which come from heaven, or those that wander dug from the earth, or flowing free by nature, bright, purifying, speeding to the ocean, here let those Waters, Goddesses, protect me".

– RIG VEDA 7.49.2

*Dedicated to the three most important women
in my life:*

*Radhamma (Radha), My mother with her
amniotic water, I breathed into life.*

*Sumati (Ummiyamma) My aunt, who fuelled
my journey and soared my imagination through
fables and fantasies of water.*

*Ambica, my wife, who traversed with me through
all my ups and downs like flowing water.*

Contents

Prologue   11

Part I: WATER: Where It All Begins...   **23**

1. Mystic Revelation   25

2. A Farmer's Wisdom   30

3. Many Mysteries of Water   36

4. Memory – The Name of Water   48

5. Water – A Different Phase   60

6. Water – A Weird Structure   69

7. Water – An Alien Substance   84

8. Water: The creator of Life   92

9. Countless Religions, Counting on Water   97

10. Water – The Divine Mother   101

11. Water – Ultimate Purifier 118

12. SHARIAH – Way to The Water Hole 131

13. Water TAO 141

14. WATER: Earthly & Heavenly 148

15. Water Character 159

16. Water & Our Generation 166

Part II: Water – Ideas for life **173**

1. As You Sow So Shall You Reap 175

2. Body of Water 182

3. The Flowing Water 189

4. Brainstorming 203

5. Dehydration – Physical and Mental 212

6. Medicinal Water 219

7. A Different Perspective 233

8. Water – Ideas for Life (WIL): An Introduction 251

9. Water – Ideas for Life (WIL):
How Pure Is My Water? 256

10. Water – Ideas for Life: Energizing Water 266

11. Water – Ideas for Life:
Cautious & Conscious Drinker 279

12. Water – Ideas for Life: Healthy Drinker 294

13. Water – Ideas for Life: Meditation & Water 302

14. Water – Ideas for Life: Being Water 313

15. Where it All Begins & Ends... 326

Acknowledgements 337

References 343

Prologue

"Its good to leave each day behind,
like flowing water, free of sadness.
Yesterday is gone and its tale told,
Today new seeds are growing."

— Rumi

A soothsayer from my village once said that my life would come to an end when I turn 22. Growing up in a traditional and religious Hindu family in Vazhoor, a picturesque village in Kerala, the soothsayer's predictions were bound to have a tremendous effect.

My God-fearing family and relatives regularly performed various rituals for the Almighty to show mercy on me and let me live longer. With limited resources and tough living conditions, I grew up with equal doses of anxiety and frustration about my life. As my prayers were never answered, my belief in God slowly eroded.

In the later stages of my life, I gradually developed an interest in atheism, which completely pulled me towards it. I couldn't care less either about the soothsayer or anybody's opinion and became an atheist.

It was the summer of April 1998. The financial capital of Mumbai was scorching hot. I left Jawaharlal Nehru Port Trust (JNPT) - India's largest container port - one afternoon. I was exhausted and thirsty. I felt my body was ridden with waves of pain thanks to a fortnight of hectic days at work. I just wanted to complete the 14-day assignment to prove to myself that I can still take on challenges.

A short stint at entrepreneurship had set me back by a huge loss. I truly didn't own anything at that point. There was nothing left to lose as well. Hence, I willed my body and mind to work on this project without taking any breaks. Needless to say, my health began deteriorating rapidly.

At the port, the heat and the humidity muddled up with the balmy Arabian Sea breeze worsened my health. After a fortnight of discomfort and with the help of some over-the-counter medicine, I was able to complete my work and now I just wanted to reach my apartment.

I took the shuttle bus and reached the intersection where I usually flag down an autorickshaw (three-wheeler vehicle commonly used in India for public commute) to my apartment. The sickness hit me like a ton of bricks as I was about to cross the road. I somehow managed to get to the other side of the street but was unable to move further. It felt as if I was intoxicated. My senses began to shut down, and suddenly I could not see, talk, or walk.

Was this how death felt? I was all of 22. Funny enough, how forgotten things of the past starts flashing right in front of your eyes even as you are passing out. The soothsayer's prediction was my last thought before crashing onto the hard pavement of Mumbai City.

I was later informed that I was lying unconscious for hours on the roadside. An onlooker who recognised me informed my friends who took me to the nearby hospital. There, I was diagnosed with the last stage of jaundice and associated complications. The doctors said that there was absolutely no hope for survival. I spent my hours at the hospital staring into the abyss. A couple of my Mumbai friends were so afraid of my condition that they decided to send me back to Vazhoor, so I could breathe my last alongside my family. My kin took me from one hospital to another trying every possible way to save me.

While at home, I tried anything and everything all at once, from Allopathy to Ayurveda to alternate healing and so on, but nothing could guarantee my survival. My condition was serious enough for the doctors to tell my family to inform my near and dear ones. In fact, one of the doctors gave in to my mother's persistence and gave her medicine for just two days as he was convinced, I wouldn't last any longer than that.

I always consider myself fortunate to have two mothers - *Radhamma* and *Sumati* - one biological and the other my aunt (mother's sister) whom I lovingly called *'Ummiamma'*. She was a widow and had been with us since my childhood. *Ummiamma* and *Radhamma* had no doubts about my recovery and harnessed all their energies to ensure my survival.

I was advised complete bed rest as that was the only way I could heal myself. I was forced not to put my body through any kind of exertion because my blood was contaminated with excess bilirubin, and I had to limit the functioning of my liver to a bare minimum. In short, I became a vegetable who could only think and see, and my existence shrunk to my bed and the four walls of the room for the next few weeks.

It was imperative for me to drink as much water as possible and bathe six to eight times a day as my body had to be kept as cold as possible. Whenever I needed water, *Ummiamma* would take some water from a small pot, put it in front of *'Nilavilakku'* (a traditional oil lamp used in houses in Kerala while offering prayers), chanted something for a couple of minutes and gave it to me. Whenever she bathed me, she used the water with some petals and leaves, and constantly murmured chants looking at the water.

There are no words to describe what I was undergoing during that difficult period. When death stares at you in your face, your entire belief system is shaken to the core, and you desperately grasp straws to remain alive.

Death is very vindictive and slow death is even more so malicious. You are tormented with the knowledge of slowly proceeding towards your end. Stripped of all emotions, the only thing that drives you is fear, a deep fear to be alive, and it helps if somebody is around to put you at ease.

Ummiamma and *Radhamma* were such people for me. Their constant presence was very reassuring during this dark phase of my life.

Miraculously, I lived past the two-day survival deadline. The following days were filled with treatments, rituals, and prayers. To cut a long story short, I survived and was given a clean chit of good health within four months. Till date, I am clueless as to how I cheated death and returned to the lands of the living. Was it unconditional love? Prayers? Medicine? Fear? I do not have an answer to this astonishing feat.

One evening, as I engaged in conversation with *Ummiamma,* my curiosity was piqued by the strange practices she had done. Believing in something that nobody was willing to believe, she went ahead with the rituals, water therapy, and prayers. I began to recognise its power, at least on a psychological level.

"Unshakeable faith and dedication can move mountains," is what we have always heard. I wanted to satisfy my curiosity and started bombarding *Ummiamma* with my questions.

"Why were you so sure about my survival?"

"Why did you frequently pour water on me and pray?"

"Were you chanting to the water?"

Her strange reply left me wonderstruck. "Son, believe me, you are made of water and water is God. It can protect you and absolve you of sins and diseases. Water can give you life because life begins and exists in water. I was very sure about this, and I used the power of water to heal you."

I just laughed. Feeling a sense of pity for her complete faith in such a common element. Little did I know that this common element was way beyond my common sense.

I returned to Mumbai after seven months and began searching for a job. A brand-new chapter in my life started when I accidentally found a job in a water treatment firm. Thanks to the nature of my job, I found myself working across various regions in India and even travelled to more than 30 countries for the commissioning of treatment plants.

Water treatment plants require a certain level of training for their day-to-day operation, and it was my responsibility to conduct training sessions for a gamut of operators, engineers, and chemists. Slowly, I started learning water's chemical, physical, and biological aspects, and its various treatment methods.

Quickly, I realised that talking about the details of the physical, chemical, and biological treatment aspects of water was mind-numbing and dry as sawdust. Neither the audience nor I would be interested in listening to such boring technical lectures. I aimed to make the training section a bit more interesting so that people were able to focus on learning about the plant operation without falling asleep!

Thus, began my hunt for water-related stories. I wanted to make my training sessions livelier by interspersing the sessions with stories and anecdotes about the various aspects of water. I took some anecdotes from *Ummiamma* and *Radhamma* and went through ancient medicinal write-ups, religious books, magazines, and even scientific papers. The more I searched, the more water revealed itself to me.

I started discussing water with many people and found myself getting more involved in the research. My respect for water grew, and today I am aware of the power of this element. Multiple discussions and discoveries became rewarding, and consequently, I started loving my profession. I was convinced beyond doubt that water is not an ordinary liquid.

Years have passed, and the insights I have gained about this precious element are thoroughly woven into the fabric of my personal and professional life. It might sound strange coming from a former atheist, but I use water as my Bible, Bhagwat Gita, and Qur'an.

I do not claim to be cured by water. My recovery may be due to several reasons beyond comprehension. Medicines, prayers, confidence, faith, love - it can have multiple labels. But undeniable truth prevails -- the extraordinary power of water cannot be explained in simple terms.

Ummiamma and *Radhamma* intuitively understood and believed in it, and so have the religions and communities for centuries, as well as all other living organisms. I have finally gained an understanding of the untold power of water, and I must share it with others too.

There are more than five million professionals who currently work in various fields of water. This book is not about water treatment, its conservation or how to solve water-related problems. I lack the credentials of a scientist, researcher, or technologist to write with a sense of authority on these subjects.

This book is a compilation of my extensive research conducted over the years. This book is my way of revealing the simple, yet complicated mysteries and secrets of water. This is my homage and devotion to water!

To enjoy your reading experience, I would like to give you a basic understanding of what science and faith mean to me.

In my perspective, science embodies duality - the known and the unknown. After decades of countless experiments and extensive research, a portion of the unknown has unfolded and become familiar to us today. Yet, science does not provide all answers. And most of the time, logic, theology, and philosophy will come to the rescue. We want everything to be concluded either scientifically, logically, theologically, or philosophically.

But irrespective of the logical and scientific findings, a third dimension persists. A reality that eludes our comprehension. There is something we don't know. It stands as unknowable, defying categorisation through logic, philosophy, theology, or science. Our logical mind will never understand it, we can only intuitively experience it. Water is one such mystery among them.

We can scientifically understand water's physical, chemical, and biological properties. Logically we can conclude the birth, behaviour, and journey of water. We can philosophically conclude the existence and transformation of water. Even then, it will still fall short of a comprehensive understanding. No one can understand it completely. Water invites us not to dissect it fully but rather to experience it.

I believe science, and faith are always right in their perspectives. Science is everyone's truth. Faith is someone's truth. Despite their viewpoints, they coexist within a larger framework. Both are divided but remain part of one circle. Two arcs formed with different perspectives but have one purpose: The promotion of well-being.

However, the relationship between science and faith is often problematic. Faith, logic, and philosophy don't require tangible proof. They are concluded in their own ways. But science is always against that conclusion. Science demands facts, evidence, and proof. Hence, both are in a prolonged cold war.

But for a proper understanding of the concept of water, we should acknowledge both. Two arcs facing opposite sides will not serve the real purpose. But when we can understand that both science and faith contribute to a complete understanding, the arcs will be on face to face, and the circle is complete. To understand the mysteries and complexities of water, we require a collaborative approach.

Many aspects discussed in this book defy scientific proof. Some conclusions may elude logical or philosophical reasoning. Some are based on science, logic, and philosophy, while others are grounded in mythology and faith. Embracing this diversity allows us to comprehend water in its entirety. Still, the third aspect of water is beyond our comprehension.

This book is about telling various dimensions of water; the scientific, the logical, the philosophical, the mythical and the unknown. This will ensure that your circle of understanding will be complete in all aspects, and you will know water's entireness beyond its boundaries drawn by us humans.

Religions understood it. So did medicinal practices. Homoeopathy, Ayurveda, and Naturopathy embraced it. Philosophers, mystics, spirituality, and science absorbed it. Now, it's time for you to dive into this mystical and complex world of water!

Let's begin our understanding of where it all begins...

"idam apah pra vahata yat kim ca durtam mayi

Yad vaham abhidudroha yad va sepa utanrtam"

"Whatever sin is found in me, whatever evil I have wrought.

If I have lied or falsely sworn, waters, remove it far from me."

— *RIG VEDA 1.23.22*

PART – I

WATER: Where It All Begins…

*"Water is everything" – **Thales***

Chapter 1

Mystic Revelation

"The water tells none of its secrets".

— Nikos Engonopoulos

Krishna Dvaipayana was the son of sage Parashara and fisherwoman Satyavati. One fateful day, Parashara was crossing the river Yamuna in Satyavati's boat. However, what began as an ordinary journey takes an unexpected turn. As the sage laid eyes upon Satyavati, desire stirred within him. Overwhelmed by a force he could not resist; Parashara confessed his intentions to Satyavati.

Satyavati, being a smart woman, knew that she could not tie down this sage into a relationship. Sensing the sage's powerful aura and supernatural abilities, she agreed to fulfil his desires under two conditions. First, she should get her virginity back, and second, the child born out of their union should be gifted in every manner possible with eternal fame. Parashara possessed many divine powers and agreed to fulfil both conditions that she had put forth. Krishna Dvaipayana was born out of this rare union.

Due to his extraordinary birth, Krishna Dvaipayana was gifted with knowledge and wisdom. He was widely respected and possessed deep knowledge and understanding of the Vedic hymns. According to Hinduism, Vedic chants are transmitted directly from the Gods and given to the people to understand their purpose in life and karma. These chants are composed and recited in a language that is considered archaic today. You need somebody knowledgeable enough to intercept and understand the meanings of these hymns. Saints and Pandits who know Vedic chants are respected, considered powerful, and highly conversant. Krishna Dvaipayana was gifted with an understanding beyond excellence.

As time unfolded, River Saraswati, one of the largest and most powerful divine rivers of the ancient Sindhu (Indus) Valley Civilisation, was almost on the verge of drying up. Krishna Dvaipayana knew that this very incident could collapse the fabric of the Indus Valley Civilisation. He decided to preserve the divine chants so that they could enlighten humanity for the times to come. He compiled the chants into four forms which are known as the four Vedas, namely, Rig, Yajur, Sama and Atharva. These Vedas are considered the oldest and most sacred manuscripts in Hinduism. Since Krishna Dvaipayana was the one who compiled them, he earned the moniker of 'Veda Vyasa'.

After years of drought, Saraswati River started flowing again, rain arrived, the Civilisation survived, and everything came back to normalcy. Veda Vyasa set forth to spread the Vedas but realised that though the common folk aspired to learn them, they found the Vedas to be very difficult to comprehend.

He chose the most popular method of sharing knowledge in those days, the art of storytelling. He decided to craft an epic tale that would encapsulate the essence of Vedas. He envisioned a narrative populated by diverse beings and personalities, each reflecting the principles of karma.

Once he was ready with his narrative, Veda Vyasa went in search of a transcriber and approached the Gods themselves. He was advised by Gods in heavenly realms that Ganapathy (Lord Ganesha), the elephant-headed God, would be the ideal transcriber for this ambitious mission. Ganapathy agreed to write this epic.

This epic has been re-told by the bard and storytellers across the Asian continent for several millennia. With numerous retellings, several plots and subplots have been added and removed today to this epic. Although it diverges from the original narrative, it still is the largest epic in the world, the *Mahabharata*. One of the best-known and famous Hindu texts, the Bhagavad Gita is also part of the *Mahabharata*.

When Ganapathy started writing the epic, he made a unique request to Veda Vyasa. He asked the sage to narrate the entire epic in one continuous flow, without any interruption, so that he could capture the emotions, action, plots, and characters precisely as intended. Veda Vyasa agreed, but he expressed his concerns to Ganapathy.

He asked, "O Lord, this story is like the mighty River Saraswathi. Its tributaries and distributaries comprise thousands of words with plots and several subplots. Like the Saraswathi which quenches the country, this epic is intended to quench the spiritual aspiration of everyone who reads it. I can narrate the epic in one attempt, but how am I going to review it to ensure that whatever I told is perfect and does justice to karma which is the essence of this epic."

Ganapathy and Veda Vyasa were seated under the shade of a century-old banyan tree at the bank of an overflowing river. Ganapathy observed the rhythmic movement in the river momentarily, took his *kamandal* (a small copper vessel to carry water) and went to the river. He collected water in his *kamandal* and placed it between him and Veda Vyasa.

Fig-1 Transcribing Mahabharata

Ganapathy replied, "Your worry is solved and now you can continue with your narration."

Puzzled, Vedavyasa said, "O, Lord. I am afraid; I am unable to comprehend why you kept the *Kamandal* with water between us."

Ganapathy smiled and said, "The water which has always been respected and revered has many supernatural powers which no other liquid or substance has on earth. Water is having memory. It can store information from its surroundings. With my divine power, I can retrieve the information stored in the water."

Thus, thousands of years ago, at the bank of a river and under the sheltering branches of an ancient banyan tree, the first-ever memory device was introduced to humanity.

Chapter 2

A Farmer's Wisdom

"Water is the driving force of all nature."

– Leonardo da Vinci

Despite my busy travel schedule, I make it a point to visit Vazhoor, my village multiple times a year and, catch up with my neighbours. A good majority of them are farmers, who work throughout the day in fields. To relax themselves in the evening, they drink toddy (a mild alcoholic drink taken from coconut or toddy palm) or arrack from a nearby town. Later they head to buy necessities for the next day and call it a night. These are simple people whose day begins and ends following the same routine every day.

Whenever I visit my village, I like to spend time with them. Our meetings include picking up a topic for the day alongside a couple of bottles of freshly fermented toddy alongside snacks. It was, and still, my way of familiarizing myself with my village and staying updated with what's happening. Once they are under the influence of toddy, the conversations vary from solemn to ridiculous. They sing, dance, tease, mimic, and sometimes pick up some random topic and debate. I look forward to these moments. Always!

One fine day, the topic was my profession. It started when they asked, "What are you doing? What job are you into?"

"I am into the treatment of water. I sell water treatment plants." I replied.

"What kind of water treatment? Do you sell water in bottles and pouches?"

"No. I treat and remove contaminants from water so that water can re-use or discharge it."

"Why? Water is always pure. Why do you want to treat it with your machine?." one asked curiously.

I started explaining how water could be contaminated and how we can treat it. I started explaining the basics of water treatment and the discussion went on. Finally, it came to sewage treatment.

"Oh! So, you treat shit as well!!", one of them smirked.

Suddenly one person from the group, Narayanan responded, "No, he takes all shit out of the water".

Narayanan is a simple farmer who toils all day in the field. Everybody in our village knew that he was adept at his work and loved all kinds of chores related to farming. He respected nature and used to converse with trees and plants! And people from my village believe that if he planted a tree or vegetable, it would grow healthier.

He continued.

"Suresh is taking the shit out of the water. Friends! You know, water is pure. It helps you survive. Years ago, I used to live for days only on water because I didn't have enough money to feed myself. But still, I never fell ill, caught any disease, or felt hungry. Somehow, water sensed my poverty and acted accordingly".

"He is high... don't let him drink anymore" joked one. Narayanan looked at him angrily and continued.

"You fool, you don't know anything. In the morning, when you put sugar and tea leaves in water and drink, you get a sweet taste. Evening, when you put alcohol in water and drink, you get intoxicated. One day when you don't have money, you will mix poison in your drinking water, and die. Water has nothing to do with it. It is people like you who put shit in the water. According to whatever shit you put; you suffer. That is what is happening today and people like Suresh make money out of it in the name of treatment". He paused for a second, looked at me and continued.

"But you don't know what is happening to this water. How it will feel..."

"Oh, so now water has feelings! I think I have to get another drink. This is unbelievable". one responded while others shook their heads.

"Yes. Every living thing including water has feelings. I have observed it many times. When I pass by an area that has a tree or a plant which I sowed; I talk to them. I know they feel the same because the water has given them the power to feel." said Narayanan with pride.

"My Gosh".

"Yes Suresh, I know I am not an educated person like you. But with whatever little knowledge I possess, I try to observe and have found many things."

"What?"

"You see that banyan tree?"

"Yes"

"It is almost 150 years old. Each leaf of a tree, every part of it has water. In my school, I learned that the roots of the trees absorb water. It travels through the bark and spans across its height distributing water to each and every part of the tree. This water is then stored there, because of which they survive. That banyan tree has also survived 150 years because of this".

I agreed as it was common knowledge.

"Yes. It is. My point is to not that". Narayanan continued

"In our school, we studied gravity. Because of gravity, we are able to walk. If we throw a stone up, it will come down because of gravity, Newton became a world-renowned scientist since he proved this. Because there is gravity, the water must move downwards only. Isn't it?"

"Yes, "everyone agreed while listening carefully.

"Then how is it possible for water to defy gravity and reach the leaves on top of the tree scaling several metres above the ground? How is it possible to find a path inside a tree which is very hard and can't break easily".

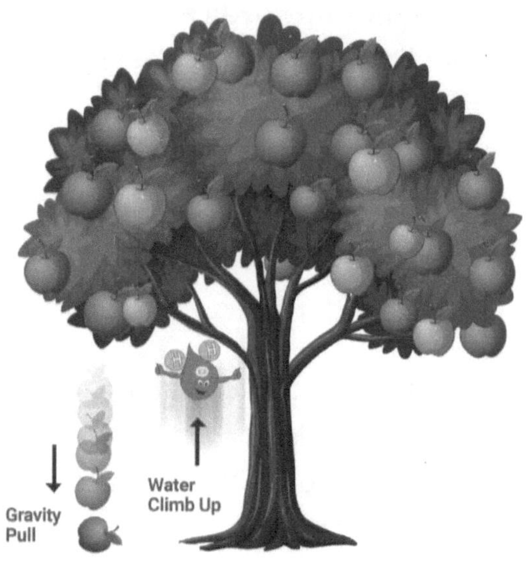

Fig: 2 Water defies gravity

"It is because of certain capillary action and surface tension of the water". I replied.

"Maybe. But how does a simple water get this unusual character? Who gives it?". He argued.

I didn't have an answer. I knew water, H_2O, is made up of two hydrogen and one oxygen atoms. It was a matter of curiosity as to how this water reached the top of the tree. How does water get this peculiar property? How it overcomes the gravitational pull. How will it pave its way inside a tree which is very hard?

"Water has a unique ability which is not understood. That's why we pray and respect it. It is divine".

Looking around at everyone with an eerie smile, Narayan gulped the remaining toddy down his throat.

I came back and resumed my work. I was in an altered state of mind. I was unhappy that I wasn't able to explain it to them properly. Even I never notice such a vital thing. I was proudly telling everyone that I am an expert in water treatment possessing good knowledge about all aspects of water. But I could neither explain how water got this peculiar nature nor understand what Narayanan told me. It hurt my ego.

Chapter 3

Many Mysteries of Water

*"Water is H2O, hydrogen two parts, oxygen one,
but there is also a third thing, that makes it water,
and nobody knows what that is."*

– D. H. Lawrence

One day, my son Harsh Vardhan and I were having a good time at Marina Beach in Chennai. Harsh is a water baby and loves to play at the beaches. As he was only a little over three years old, I used to be alert whenever he went near the shore to play with waves. I would often be with him. However, that day, I was wearing denims and didn't want to get into the water. I was walking a little away from the shore and asked Harsh to walk with me too. But he refused and told me, "No Dadda! I want to walk here!"

"Why?" I asked.

"My feet sink in the sand over there but not here" He innocently replied.

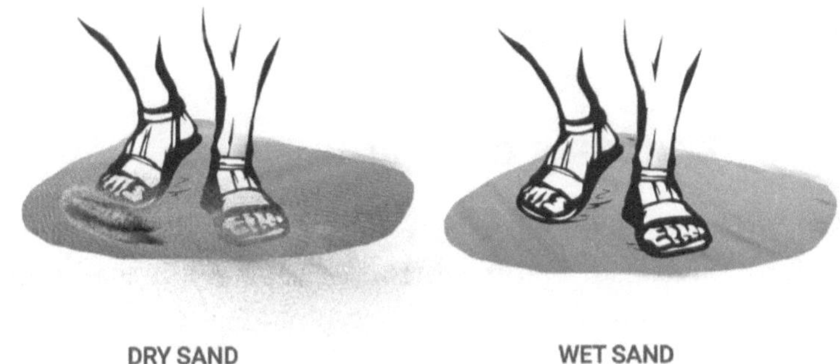

Fig 3-Feet sink in dry sand, not in wet sand

Suddenly, something crossed my mind, and I observed the wet and dry sand one after the other. I had been to this beach several times, but I never noticed this phenomenon. When we were walking on the dry sand, our feet were sinking which made it difficult to walk on it. But when we were on the wet sand, our feet gave us a firm grip. How? My knowledge and experience were not able to comprehend it.

Three incidents have altered my perspective on water - one which you read in the prologue about my illness and survival, second the drunk chat with Narayanan, and then the sand phenomena which I noticed at Marina Beach, thanks to Harsh.

These initial experiences made me convinced that there is something beyond my understanding of water which includes its physical, biological, chemical, and thermal properties. I decided to spend a good amount of time researching water and its properties beyond physical, chemical, and biological aspects. The more I researched, the more the water revealed itself to me. In fact, this made me more conscious about water and my interactions with it on a day-to-day basis.

Many Mysteries of Water

In our day-to-day life, we may come across the following questions related to water which do not have a readymade answer from our logical minds.

Why does water store heat better than any other fluid?

How can two atoms of hydrogen and one of oxygen - both flammable gases combine and form a liquid? Not another gas.

Why does water have unusually high melting and boiling points?

Why does ice float?

Why does hot water freeze faster than cold water?

Why does warm water vibrate longer than cold water?

Why does the structure of water change at high temperatures?

Why does water shrink on melting?

Why is it that the surface of water is denser than the rest?

How can a diaper hold so much water?

Why does water get stored in a wounded area?

Why are water clouds separated and not joined together?

Why is a raindrop having an approximate round shape?

Why do drops of water stick to surfaces?

Why do water droplets bounce?

How does water create a lubrication effect between bone joints?

All liquids become more viscous under pressure, but why does cold water get runny when it is squeezed?

Some of the questions are still unanswered while some are beyond comprehension. The mysteries lie with water itself with much more yet to come.

Water is a remarkable substance that exhibits several anomalies, setting it apart from any other liquids. These anomalies play a crucial role in supporting life on Earth and have significant implications for our various natural processes. We don't even know what is happening deep down in the ocean and inside the earth. What we know is still the tip of the iceberg, with the rest waiting to be unravelled.

There are 64 anomalies documented so far with water and some scientists believe it is more than 70. The anomalies of water contribute to the ecological balance and sustainability of our planet, influencing climate patterns, supporting diverse ecosystems, and playing a central role in biochemical processes.

Let us begin our understanding with some of the anomalies of water.

Water expands with the decrease in temperature

Have you ever noticed that when you fill water in ice plates and keep it in the freezer, ice starts expanding? The volume of ice is larger than the volume of water you have poured. Why does water expand, instead of contracting, when it freezes?

In everyday terms, thermal expansion is a universal occurrence for all substances. When atoms heat up, they jiggle around more exuberantly and due to this, they occupy more spaces, causing expansion. Similarly, in cooler temperatures, atoms arrange themselves in a more orderly fashion, occupying less space. This will increase the density and contraction.

Every liquid contracts as the temperature decreases. That's why we can store LPG (Liquified Petroleum Gas) of 16 kg in a movable cylinder. Once this liquid gas is released into the atmosphere, the temperature rises and volume increases. All other gases behave in the same way. When temperature reduces it becomes liquid and compresses. That's why natural gas can be transported to various parts of the world in compressed liquid form and at the user point it releases approximately 50 times higher volume than what is stored.

But for water, it works exactly the opposite. Water has a different structure. Water expands when temperature decreases. Similarly, water freezes fast when it is hot. Next time, when you want to freeze water quicker than normal, just heat it and then put it in the fridge. You can make ice cubes faster.

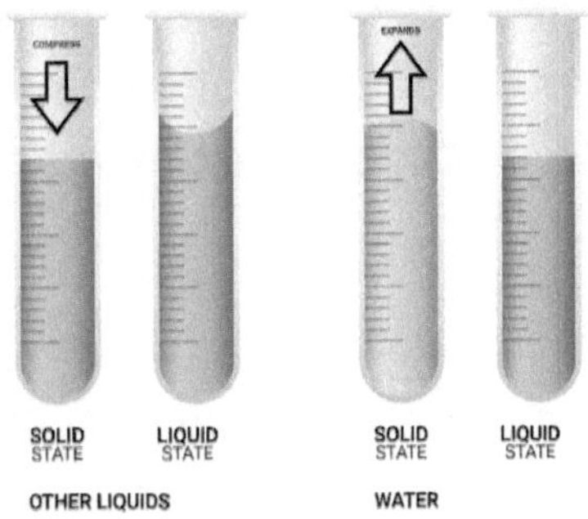

Fig-4 – Water expands in solid state

Floating ice, saving lives

We know that the solid state of most things is much denser than the liquid state and hence they sink. But water behaves differently. In the winter season, in many parts of the world, the temperature is sub-zero. Water bodies freeze. What would happen to the fish and other living organisms if all the water bodies were frozen? Obviously, they will not survive.

There comes another mysterious design. Water in its solid state is less dense than its liquid state which means water at 4° Celsius is denser than water at 0° Celsius, which is ice. Because ice is less dense than water, it floats. This permits life to survive safely under the sheets of ice during freezing winter.

In lakes, ponds and other water bodies, the denser water sinks below less-dense water. Even when ice is formed on its topmost layer, water beneath the ice is not frozen and this is what protects the life beneath from dying. Water is highly dense at 4°C but when the temperature goes below this, the density reduces. This phenomenon of maximum density of water and low density of ice results in the compulsion of a body of freshwater which is close to 4°C before any freezing can occur.

We can observe the freezing of vegetable oils during winter. These oils start freezing from bottom to top. However, in rivers, lakes and oceans, water freezes from top to bottom, thus paving the way for the survival of the marine ecology. This insulates the water from further freezing by reflecting sunlight into space and allowing rapid thawing. If water was densest at its freezing point, then in winter, the very cold water at the surface of lakes would sink, and the lake could freeze from the bottom, making it impossible for the survival of life underneath. Instead, water protects its ecology by being a good insulator of heat.

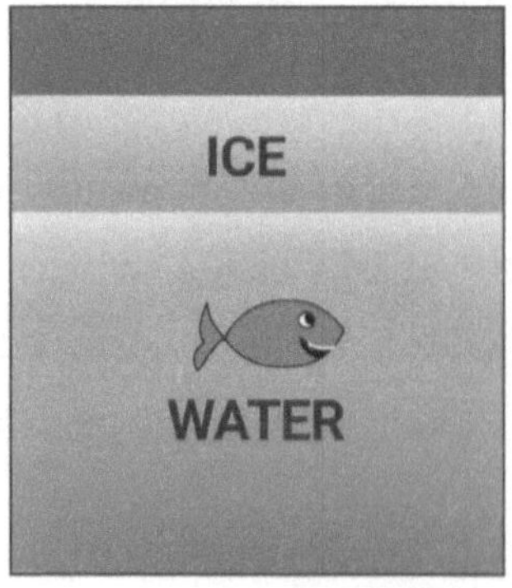

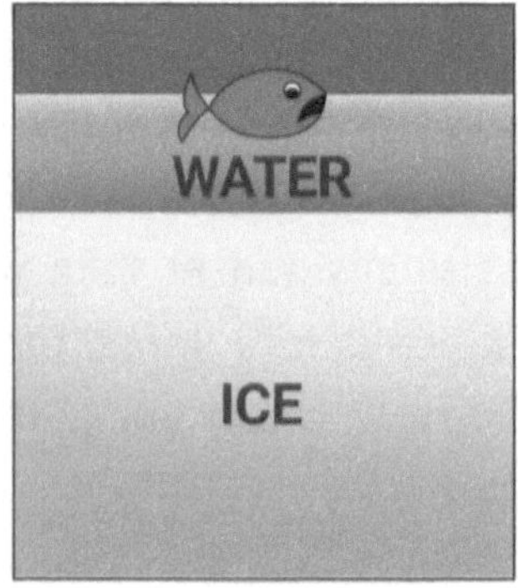

Fig-5 Water saving marine lives in winter because Ice floats

A firefighting liquid consists of two flammable gases

As we all know, two atoms of hydrogen and one atom of oxygen combine to form water. However, both hydrogen and oxygen are flammable gases. But water is used for fighting and controlling fire. All fire engines are filled with water. The basic firefighting technique is nothing but sprinkling water onto the fire to control it. It is an astonishing fact that two flammable gases combined can extinguish fire.

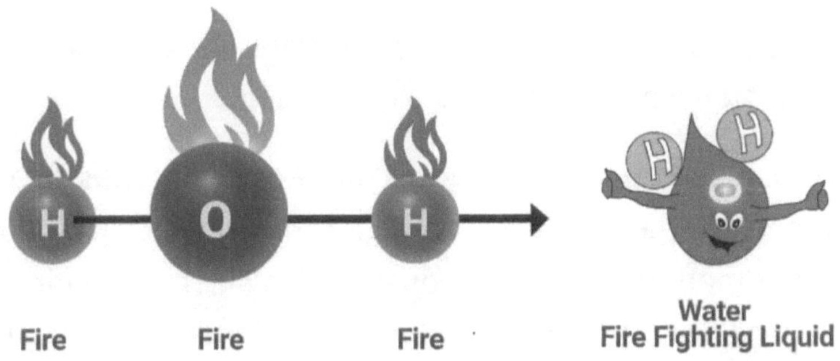

Fig-6 Fire +Fire = Water – A firefighting liquid

Can water be created in the lab? It's not so simple

If the water is so simple and consists of only two atoms of hydrogens and one atom of oxygen, then why are we not able to make water in our labs and factories? Both hydrogen and oxygen are easily available, and our water scarcity can be tackled to some extent if we can make lab water.

In theory, it looks easy. But is it not that simple because hydrogen and oxygen molecules don't spontaneously form water. It requires a high amount of energy to make little water. Also, it releases a lot of energy during the reaction. The more water you generate this way, the more heat and light are produced, and an explosion-like situation could take place. A strange behaviour, isn't it?

A blade that can cut metals

I was engulfed with disbelief when I first heard that water can be compressed and used for cutting metal. Water is pushed out at tremendous speed through a tiny hole to cut through everything from metal to ceramics to plastics.

Today, it is one of the most preferred methods to cut materials that are sensitive to high temperatures generated by other methods. In many industries ranging from mining to aerospace, to shipbuilding, water is used for cutting, shaping, carving, and reaming. Even a small quantity of water can break the hardest rock.

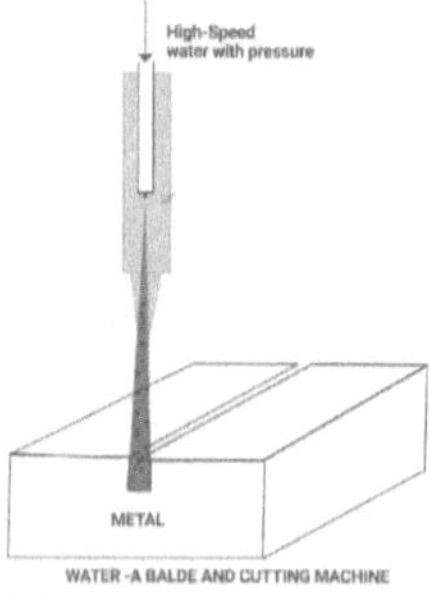

Fig-7 Water — A cutting machine

Pure water – no electrical shock

Pure water has a neutral pH of 7. It is neither acidic nor alkaline. It doesn't conduct electricity, which means you will not get an electric shock when you pass current through pure water. It's the substances and minerals dissolved in water that conduct electricity.

Fig-8 Pure water – no electric shock

You can mix anything

Water is called the "universal solvent" because it dissolves more substances than any other liquid. The perfect interaction of water molecules with the molecules of other substances makes water a universal solvent. This quality of water is important to every living thing on Earth. Adhesion and cohesion are other properties that every water molecule on Earth possesses. These properties make molecules of water and other substances stick to each other. This means that wherever water goes, either through the ground or through our bodies, it takes along valuable chemicals, minerals, and nutrients, making it the perfect universal solvent found in nature.

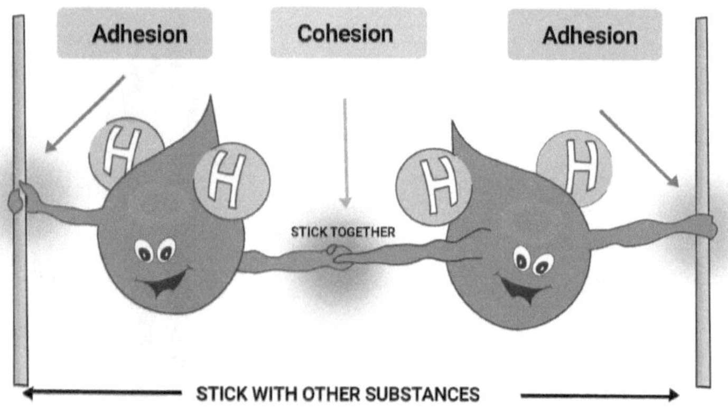

Fig-9 Adhesion and Cohesion of water

Cooling water

There are a lot of discussions that happen around heat and water. Water has a high specific heat index.[1] It absorbs a lot of heat before it begins to get hot. This is why water is valuable to many industries as a cooling agent. To give you a daily life example, water is generally used as a coolant in cars. Water has to gain a great amount of heat to get hot as compared to

---

1   The heat index, also known as the apparent temperature, is **what the temperature feels like to the human body when relative humidity is combined with the air temperature.**

other liquids. The high specific heat index of water also helps regulate the rate at which air changes temperature. This is the reason why the temperature change between seasons is gradual rather than sudden, especially near the oceans.

The above factors are only a small portion of water behaviours. Many facts are quite amusing. You will read more about such factors and circumstantial behaviours of water in the following chapters. No liquid behaves quite as oddly as water. It exhibits a raft of unusual behaviours.

All that we discussed above, points to one major aspect of water. The supernatural power which water holds is beyond conventional scientific explanations. Water is the most omnipresent substance on our planet. Life as we know, cannot exist without water. Yet some unique properties are poorly understood.

Chapter 4

Memory – The Name of Water

—————— ❧❧ ——————

"Water has a memory and carries within it our thoughts and prayers. As you are water, no matter where you are, your prayers will be carried to the rest of the world".

– Dr. Musaru Emoto

When you visit a house in India or any other South Asian country, it is customary for them to offer water. This tradition was upheld for centuries regardless of religious beliefs. Initially, I didn't understand why they followed this custom. Later, I learned this has a meaning.

Firstly, it is a way to show respect. The other interesting reason is that they want us to carry their memories with us by drinking the water they offer. When a house is offering water to you, unknowingly they are utilizing the power of water memory.

In many houses, even today, they keep a pot of water near the place of worship so that water can absorb the good vibes during chanting, and rituals during their daily prayer. They believe, this water is divine and consuming it daily will have a positive effect on them. By further discussing this aspect, I want to take you through to the first mystery - the memory retention of water - and explore a little more about it.

For ages, our ancestors from different cultures and religions have recognized the power of memory. Medicinal systems such as Homoeopathy, Hydrotherapy, Ayurveda, Traditional Chinese and Japanese medicine techniques, and various other natural medicinal branches have originated and thrived for centuries. These medicinal branches widely use water for healing. Those days communication between one part of the world to another was not even possible and many didn't even know that another part of the globe existed. However, without any communication between them, the awareness of water memory is used and accepted with their intelligence and experience. It was beyond a logical conclusion but a tested and proven knowledge in earlier times.

Initially, scientists were not interested in doing research with water beyond its chemistry. The 18th and 19th centuries saw a rapid growth in scientific research and inventions in other areas, but water became a subject of negligence. Religious rituals used terms like "holy water", which gave some mystery to water grabbing the interest of scientists. However, they considered research on water to be either risky, boring, or not worthy. The concept of water memory was accepted more convincingly in the latter half of the 19th century, and many experiments and research took place on this subject.

Initially, in the scientific community, scientists thought water memory could be because of bacterial action or the action of some organics which inhabit the water. There were also scientific communities which thought that the memory could be because of some organic molecules trapped in the water. But soon these hypotheses were proven false.

Until the 17th century, humans believed the ocean depth to be a lifeless place, and that life existed only in some places on land and the shallow depth of the sea. But then, they went deep into the ocean, and it resulted in a revelation of a whole new world.

Researchers who studied the behaviours of aquatic animals found that sharks can recognise their prey from a distance of several hundred meters. In some movies, they show how sharks identify their prey and attack based on the blood mixed in seawater. It is absolutely clear that water is a medium that transmits scent over long distances.

Initially, researchers believed that the substances emitted by the body surface, such as mucus in fish, blood or other body waste are the reason why sharks can locate their prey at a far distance without errors. But once these substances and their scents are submerged in the seawater, they dissolve quickly. These substances will break into small parts and spread in all directions due to the constant currents in the sea. The substances which carry smell will also decrease and spread in all directions due to this.

When it comes to other creatures like hagfish, the cleaners of the sea, they behave differently. Hagfishes have very poor vision and often eat dead animals. How is a visually disabled fish able to identify dead prey? Even crabs have very poor vision, yet they can also identify dead prey very easily.

This understanding gave rise to another revelation about water. Over years of study, it was found that water was able to gather information about the death of a creature. This finding created a long controversy concerning the laws of organic chemistry.

Allow me to explain.

Lakes, ponds, and other water bodies are the water containers of the earth. They store water and are home to large numbers of bacteria and other organisms. As we know these organisms multiply due to photosynthesis and other aiding processes. You can see algae in all these water bodies. But have you seen algae in seawater?

Any organic molecules in the seawater quickly decompose into simple components such as carbon dioxide and water. This is the law of organic chemistry. When we have a wound or cut in our body, we use saline water to clean it because it is safe and is not contaminated with any microorganisms or bacteria.

Water treatment professionals and chemists know that seawater does not contain much biological oxygen demand

(BOD)[2]. If that is so, then how can water store the information based on odour or any organic substances?

After a lot of studies and research in this context, today many experts conclude that water can store information for a long time, while the creatures in the sea can collect and use the stored data. Sharks, hagfish, crabs, and many other creatures use this information for their survival.

This is one theory.

I wish to give some more details on the subject of the sea as we all know that life first originated in the sea. Another dimension of sea life is that many scientists believe that the migration routes of marine creatures are largely dependent on the complex information links stored in water for years. These living beings can navigate through the same route over and over again. They understand and use the information stored in water for making their route map. So, the laws of organic chemistry are not wrong, substances will decompose into a single compound, but water has a chemical memory that stores the information about every being that was once in it. This information remains stored for a long time.

Water memory - developments

In 1796, when Samuel Hahnemann invented Homeopathy, the largest established alternative medicine today. The

---

2   Biochemical oxygen demand (BOD) is the amount of dissolved oxygen (DO) needed (i.e. demanded) by aerobic biological organisms to break down organic material present in a given water sample at a certain temperature over a specific time period.

conventional scientific world either ignored or laughed at him. They thought it was not practical or was "witch science" or pseudoscience. Homeopathy lacked the rigour essentials of the scientific method in those days as its insight was completely different.

Homoeopathy is created based on the idea of "likes cures likes." He believed the effects of modern drugs on the body are similar for a deceased person and a healthy person. He rejected drug therapy and believed it to be harmful, irrational, and hence inadvisable.

Hahnemann believed in the power of water and started curing people by making formulations in the water without leaving any harmful traces in the human body, the whole world was astonished. He developed a technique of extreme dilution in such a way that only the effects of substances remained but not the harmful effects.

The spirit-like medicinal power gained the greatest popularity from the 19th century onwards. Even today, the secret behind homoeopathy is not completely understood but this alternative therapy is well-known in many countries.

One of the discoveries made by scientists probing the behaviour of water is polywater, discovered by Russian scientists in 1960. When they restricted water in very narrow capillary tubes, the water behaved very differently. This water was very difficult to freeze or evaporate. The density of the water was high, and molecules behaved differently. They called it "polywater," and gave a different phase altogether compared to ordinary water. However, this incident was not appreciated by some scientific community due to the limitations of the experiment and was rather considered inaccurate.

Jacques Benveniste, the French scientist was the first person to write about water memory scientifically. He experimented with water, mixed biologically active substances, and diluted it multiple times till the substances were completely removed from the water. Yet water retained the memory of the substances and behaved similarly. The effect of the substance stayed with water, even when the substance traces were absent.

He published his paper in a science magazine, and it supported the homoeopathic procedure. His further experiments attracted a lot of misconceptions, controversy, and sensation among some scientists. Later, he declared that the memory of water can be digitised, transmitted, and reinstated to another sample of water.

Dr David Schweitzer, a German scientist while doing blood analysis came across a finding that blood cells express themselves in response to situations geometrically. Not surprisingly, blood cells consist of 80 % water and blood plasma consists of 90-92% of water. His further experiments and studies concentrated on this effect.

After 10 years of effort, Dr Schweitzer was able to develop a special fluorescent microscope in 1996 that could observe small light bodies and life fluids. This enabled him to study and demonstrate how water was capable of acting as a memory system and store information in blood cells.

Dr Shweitzer noticed the particles in the water change in response to thoughts and influences. He photographed the effects and demonstrated that an activity could be directly influenced by negative and positive thoughts. He noticed that water expressed itself with a language based on geometry, colour, and shapes. This discovery was a revolution.

He later pursued more experiments with water. One of his realisations was that our brain needed certain elements to send information from one area to another. Apart from the minerals, he knew that some medium was required in between to complete this mission. He worked on the water at a specific temperature and noticed that information began to develop just before the water evaporated. Further studies showed that the development of information in water depended on the thought or situations. Water infused with positive and negative elements had separate formations. Water from different sources had different kinds of development. Each water formed a different kind of development depending upon the atmosphere it was collected in.

Meanwhile, in Japan, Dr Musaru Emoto, a doctor in alternative medicines started his research on crystal photography of water. After a long research and practice, he was able to freeze water in a particular way and take photographs of frozen crystal water. The pure water crystal turned into a beautiful hexagonal shape.

He continued with his experiment by taking the water from different sources like taps, rivers, mountains, and lakes and each photograph delivered from these sources formed a different kind of shape pattern. Water which flowed naturally gave excellent crystal photographs, but the water taken from contaminated sources produced different kinds of images. Some didn't even form any image.

His next step was to introduce water to a place where Beethoven's and Mozart's symphonies played. The images created were excellent with proper patterns and shapes. But when disturbing sounds and louder voices were played, different kinds of images were created. He then introduced words to the water and took pictures.

Words like "Thank you" and "Gratitude" resulted in images that had proper crystal formations but a word like "You fool!" resulted in an entirely different image.

Dr. Emoto's years of experiment with hundreds of images of water taken from different sources and different situations proved a point that water would behave differently depending on the circumstances.

Water collects the information from its surroundings and stores it in its memory cell. When this water was frozen and pictures were taken, the photos were nothing, but the reflection of the information stored in its memory. As per Dr Emoto's research, each water molecule carries an information system.

Dr. Bernd Kroplin conducted many experiments involving water where he explored the effect of water under various influences. He subjected dried water droplets through ultrasound, music, and mobile radiation and examined the behaviour through dark field microscopy. Each experiment gives a distinct pattern within the water droplets.

With the help of Static and Dynamics in Aerospace Constructions at the University of Stuttgart (ISD), Dr. Kroplin extended his research involving many students and diversified water sources.

Through these experiments, Dr. Kroplin underscores water's remarkable capacity to record, store and transmit information. In 2005, he published his book titled *"The World in a Drop: Memory and Forms of Thought in Water"* which shed more light on the memory narratives.

Luc Montagnier was a French virologist who lived between 1932 and 2022. He was the joint recipient of the Nobel Prize in Physiology in 2008 for his role in the discovery of HIV (Human Immunodeficiency Virus), which causes AIDS. He is also associated with the memory of water.

Montagnier's theory stated that DNA sequences can be transmitted electromagnetically to water, leaving an imprint that can supposedly be detected by highly sensitive instruments. This concept gained attention after Montagnier published a series of studies suggesting that DNA molecules could communicate with each other by emitting low-frequency electromagnetic waves that imprint themselves on surrounding water molecules.

One of the key experiments supporting Montagnier's theory involved diluting and shaking bacterial DNA in water, and then measuring the electromagnetic signals emitted by the water. According to Montagnier, these signals could be detected even after the original DNA was removed, implying that water could somehow "remember" the information it had been exposed to.

More than the physical, chemical, biological and thermal properties of water, which we can measure and analyse today, there is something beyond the understanding of many of us those results in such behaviour and anomalies of water. It is not the chemical and physical properties which decide the anomalies of water rather it is because of its structure.

Some scientists concluded that water molecules group together to form clusters. Every cluster works like a memory cell of some sort. These memory cells can store information from their surroundings and carry it with them. Depending on the situations and surroundings in which it is stored, the structure of water changes accordingly.

It is more or less like our nervous system; the water cluster behaves in the same way. It does not alter the chemical and physical compositions, but the structure changes according to the information stored in the water.

Today modern instruments have recorded that an average water memory cell will have 4,00,40,000 (40.04 million) information panels and each panel is responsible for the interaction with the environment and will act accordingly to the environment.

The "water memory" is a debated subject. In traditional scientific understanding, the properties of a substance dissolved in water are determined by its chemical composition and the interactions between its molecules. It is not by any memory-like capacity of the water. When a substance is dissolved in water, it forms a solution. The properties of that solution are influenced by the solute (the substance being dissolved), and not the water. They think the "structuration" of water could mimic the effect is impossible.

Their second valid argument is that water cannot hold its structure for a long time. It is due to the peculiar hydrogen bonding of the water. I will explain the hydrogen bond phenomena in the coming chapters.

In the exploration of "water memory", I request my readers to maintain a neutral stance and approach, neither endorsing nor dismissing any hypotheses outright. As we explore subsequent chapters, remain open-minded and allow curiosity to guide your understanding. By gaining a comprehensive view of water's complexities, you may form more informed opinions about water and its place.

Chapter 5

Water – A Different Phase

"In one drop of water are found all the secrets of all the oceans; in one aspect of You are found all the aspects of existence".

– Kahlil Gibran

Owing to my years of involvement in the water treatment industry, the second subject that fascinated me was the surface tension-related properties of water.

In my village, there is a huge peepal tree. During my childhood, we used to play hide and seek under it. Many times, the seeds from the tree would fall on us and we would stamp the seeds. It used to stain our clothes and I used to get scolded by my mother for soiling my school uniform. Sometimes, I used to take apart its seed and observe it. The peepal's seed is tiny (almost the size of a rice grain), which when planted, turns into a humungous tree over time.

When I got to know about the surface tension of water which can overcome the gravitational force of the Earth and reach the top of a tree, I was convinced of the power of water.

Water exhibits the highest surface tension compared to any other liquid. That's why, a drop of water can form a geometric shape like raindrops. Water can cut through hard rocks and metals and allow heavier objects to float on its surface due to its high surface tension. When we carefully place a needle in the water, it can float on the surface even though it is several times denser than water. The same is the case with small insects walking on the water. Soaps and detergents are normally mixed with a surfactant to reduce the surface tension of the water. This made me very curious to know about the other processes where water played a vital role.

One such process is photosynthesis, the process by which trees make food, helping the seed transform into a magnificent tree. A seed requires many things to stay alive, grow and transform into a tree. It requires carbon, minerals, water, and light. Most molecules in a seed require some kind of carbon, which comes originally from carbon dioxide. Also, a collection of other elements comes from the mineral nutrients in the soil. Seeds also use energy and nutrients stored in the soil to grow. The light and heat energy from the sun converts into chemical energy for seed growth.

Once these activities are at their peak, water plays a mysterious role that even today we do not understand fully. The water in the seeds reaches about 400 Bar pressure during the germination process and due to this phenomenon, seeds grow, and the baby shoots break the soil and pop out. A standard atmospheric pressure at sea level is 1.013 Bar and the pressure which is generated during germination is about 400 times more than atmospheric pressure. Without this process, seeds won't grow and there won't be any life for the plant. How can a simple element like water perform such a miraculous thing?

When Narayanan, the farmer in my village, discussed about how water reached up to the top of the tree overcoming the gravitation pull, he was talking about the secret of water. Let's look at it the scientific way!

The movement of water in the plants is due to the osmotic pressure and capillary action. Capillary action refers to the chemical forces that move water as a continuous film rather than individual molecules. Water molecules in the soil and plant cling to one another and don't let go. When one molecule is drawn up the plant stem, it pulls another one along with it. These forces that link water molecules together can be overcome by gravity and reach the required level of pressure to overcome gravitational force.

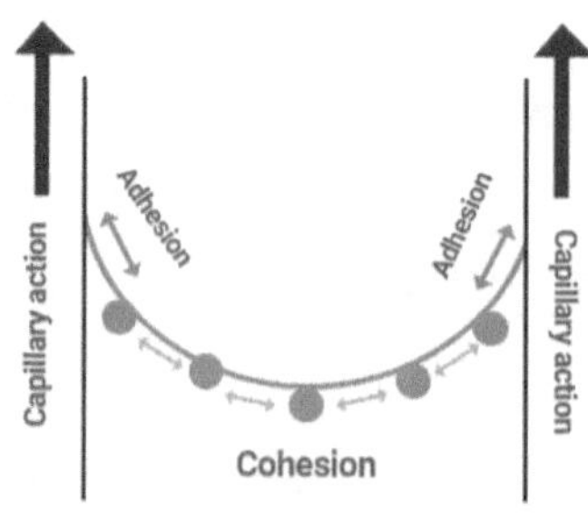

Fig-10 Water's capillary action

The water drop is composed of water molecules that like to stick together. Water has a very high surface tension. In other words, water is sticky and elastic and tends to clump together in drops rather than spread out in a thin film. Capillary action occurs when the adhesion to the walls is stronger than the cohesive forces between the liquid molecules. This phenomenon happens without any external pressure. That is the mystery.

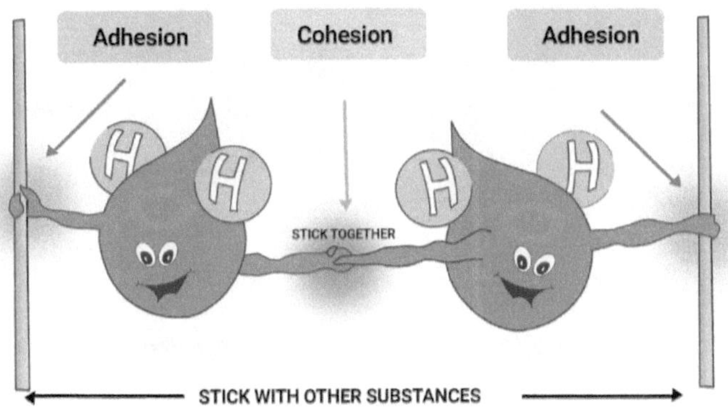

Fig-11 Adhesion & cohesion of water

It is an amazing property of water. Because of this, the plant rises out from the soil, water is transported via roots that travel through the stem and reach the topmost leaves. It can work against the gravitation force and tens of atmospheric pressure to rise within the large tree roots to reach the top. The life in plants and trees is the blessing of water.

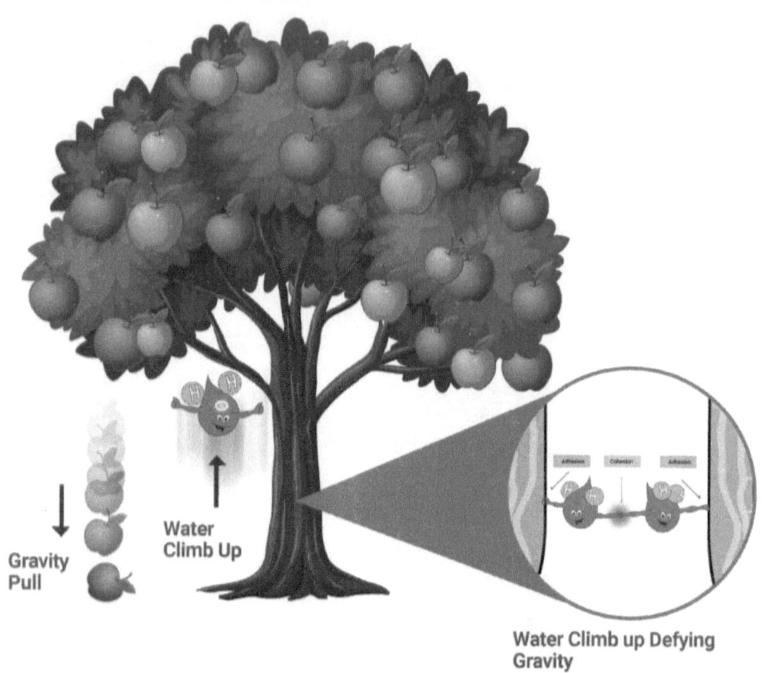

Fig-12 Water climbs up defying gravity

As the water molecule starts climbing, it pulls another water molecule along which drags other water molecules, so that they reach the top of the tree through tissues. In almost similar fashion, the blood in our body travels continuously throughout our body. Surface tension is responsible for capillary action, which allows water and its dissolved substances to move through the roots of plants and the tiny blood vessels in our bodies. Without this unique action plants, humans, and all other living organisms will not survive.

If we hunt for a proper scientific explanation of this unique property, history has many contradictory explanations to offer. The physical and chemical properties of water are extraordinarily complicated and incompletely understood. But we know one thing for sure; this phenomenon happens each time, every time, and everywhere without any external influence!

This extraordinary quality and complexity of water results in the floating ice, wet sand stability, and many other phenomena I mentioned in the initial chapters. Now the question is, how did water get these characters? As we know it is made with two atoms of hydrogen and one atom of oxygen -- a very simple composition as per chemistry.

Recently, water science has transformed into other dimensions. Many scientists have now started believing that water has a fourth state beyond solid, liquid and gas. It works beyond elementary chemistry.

About a century ago, Sir William Hardy demonstrated the existence of the fourth state, a state between the solid and liquid states of water. It is a gel-like state neither solid nor liquid.

Later, in 2013, Dr. Gerald H. Pollack wrote in his book about his findings on this fourth phase which he calls the exclusion (EZ) zone. Water has extraordinary properties in its fourth phase. When the water in its fourth phase builds, it expels all other molecules and materials, thus called the Exclusion Zone (EZ). It expelled everything and contained a lot of charges. It is surprising to note that, as per his book, the water becomes more structured at this EZ zone with more oxygen atoms.

Normally, water molecules exist in a neutral state when in the form of H_2O. Oxygen atoms have a charge of minus two (-2) and hydrogen atoms have plus one charge (+1). But under specific conditions, the interaction between hydrogen and oxygen atoms will give a special type of molecule called hydronium ion. It is the state of water having an extra hydrogen ion and the water formula in this state is H_3O.

Hydronium ions are highly mobile due to the positive moiety binds. Similarly, water also can lead to a different formation due to self-ionisation and negative moiety which is the building block of the EZ.

The formula of water at the EZ phase is H_3O_2, instead of H_2O we commonly known. During the fourth phase, water behaves very differently. It is more viscous, more stable, and more ordered in its atomic structure. The atomic structure of ice and water droplets resembles the atomic structure of EZ. Water's refractive index in the EZ phase is 10% more than normal water. Water at this phase is denser and in alkaline conditions and carries a negative charge which can hold and release the energy needed.

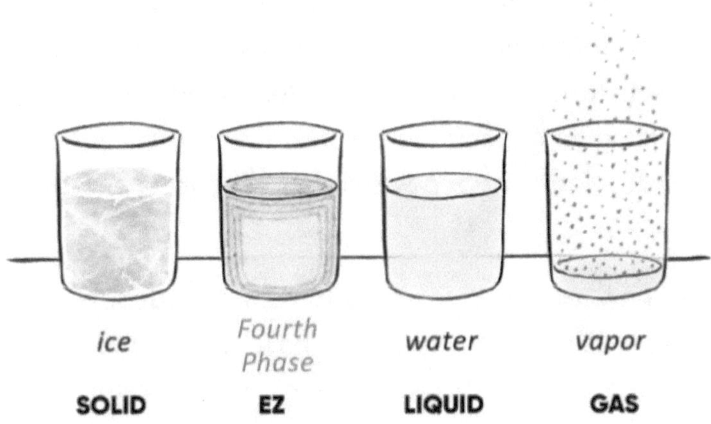

Fig-13 Fourth phase of water

One of the examples of the EZ phase given in his book is about water droplets. EZ water covers the droplets and hydronium ions fill the interior part and both will repel each other. The push-pull force of both the hydronium ion and EZ zone gives the droplet its round shape.

When droplets fall on the water's surface, they will stand there for some moments before merging due to EZ nature. Dr Pollack has elaborately described the EZ water presence in various natural occurrences such as water dribbling out of gel, cloud formations, batteries, and so on. The EZ layer of the seawater provides cohesion and upward thrust which help ships to stay afloat.

As per Dr. Pollack's findings, the creation of this EZ phase is due to light, the electromagnetic energy. It is similar to the first step of the photosynthesis process This energy received by water is either from sunlight or from infrared or ultraviolet rays. This energy splits the water molecules. We can build or convert the fourth phase of water on any water-loving surface with the help of infrared energy. Pollack and his team are now working on the commercial use of this discovery, getting into the development of desalination, producing energy from water etc.

Any new theory challenges our current understanding. Many scientists admit that we have only scratched the surface of the scientific wonders of water. Water exhibits different behaviour patterns in various situations. That's why experiments with water can give conflicting results in different scenarios. Sometimes it shows the same results, while at other times it produces different or unclear outcomes. One reason for this is the strange and complex structure of water molecules. Let's find out more about this in the upcoming chapter.

Chapter 6

Water – A Weird Structure

"Water is not simply H_2O but rather is a complex of interconnected water molecules, especially in its solid and liquid states. Moreover, this network is constantly shifting its connections (Known as hydrogen bonds) among neighbours".

— West Merlin

No liquid behaves quite as oddly as water. We can look into some physiological aspects of H_2O to understand the structural anomalies of water. This chapter is a bit more about the physical and chemical properties of water. I will try to keep it as simple as possible.

Water – A weird symmetry

We can keep aside the understanding of the fourth phase of water for the time being. Let's look into the other phases. Water is the only compound on Earth that exists in all three phases - solid, liquid and gas. Water exhibits distinctive

69

behaviours across these states. Water molecules behave differently in these states.

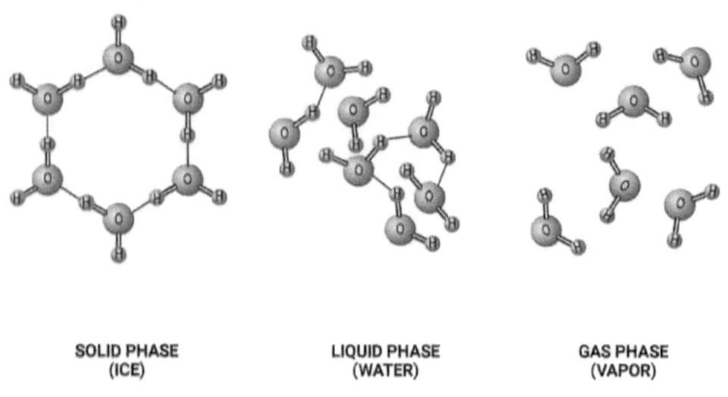

Fig-14 Water Molecules in Three States

This versatility lies in the complex structure of water molecules and their interactions with one another. As we know, water is a compound resulting from the chemical union of hydrogen and oxygen. This happens when electrons are shared, forming a covalent bond.

Molecular formations follow distinct geometric patterns, which dictate approximate bond angles around the central atom. This serves as the foundation for the geometric patterns in which molecules arrange themselves. These patterns dictate the approximate bond angles around the central atom. For example, in situations with only two electron pairs around the central atom, the bonds arrange themselves on opposite sides. This will minimize electrostatic repulsion, resulting in a linear bond angle of 180°. Similarly, three regions adopt a trigonal geometry with a bond angle of 120°, and four regions form a tetrahedral arrangement with bond angles of 109.5° and so on.

However, this conventional understanding encounters an exception with water. According to the above principles, water's geometry should be linear like carbon dioxide (CO_2), 180° apart. Surprisingly, the actual bond angle within the H-O-H molecule is 104.5°. This angle is deviating from the expected bond angle arrangement. This angle also deviates from the typical tetrahedral angles of 109.5° and the pentagon angles of 108°, adding a layer of complexity to water's molecular structure.

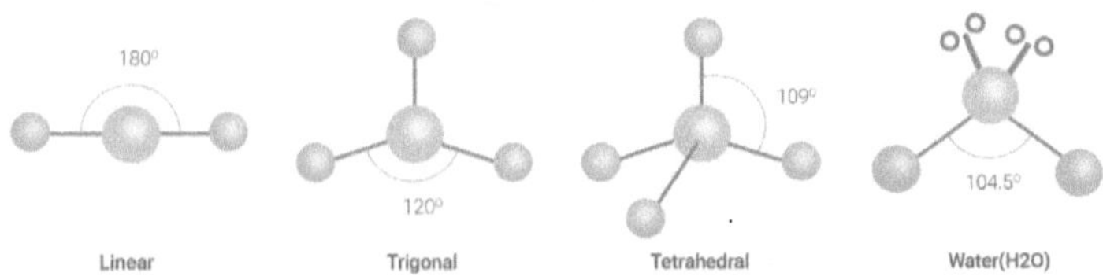

Fig-15 The distinctive angle of water

This special bond angle is unusual and unique. Like many things in the chemical world, the shape and structure of a molecule is an important determinant of its function. As I explained above, the water molecule is not linear or tetrahedron but maintains a distinctive bent shape - a weird symmetry.

Water Molecule – A crooked shape

The molecule-related surprises of water do not just end with a bend angle. When we consider a geometric angle of 104.5°, water is expected to have a V-shaped structure. But in reality, the shape of the water molecule deviates from the V-shape and adopts a distinct structure. It has four sides: two sides are with atoms and the other two are with lone pair electrons. This arrangement gives a crooked shape to water molecules.

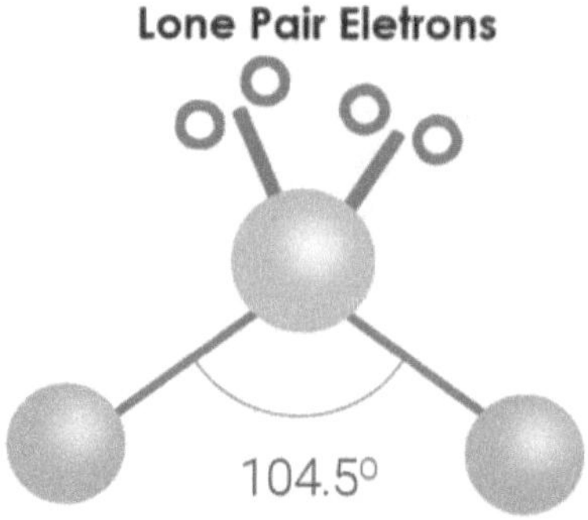

Fig-16 Crooked shape of water molecules

The lone pair electrons are from oxygen and do not participate in bonding with other atoms from the molecules. Instead, they position themselves as far away as possible. These two lone pair electrons along with two hydrogen atoms provide a geometry angle of 104.5°.

Water and the Vibrational Anomaly

As we know molecules are not static. All molecules vibrate, as in, they oscillate like a spring. When temperature increases, oscillation also increases and reduces when temperature decreases. At an absolute zero temperature of minus 273 Degrees Celsius, a negligible vibration only can be observed in any molecules. However, water molecules have a very significant vibration even at absolute zero temperatures. The scientific explanation for this phenomenon is that both hydrogen and oxygen are very light atoms and hence it retains vibrational energy to a greater extent. This anomaly challenges the conventional boundaries of molecular behaviour, casting water as a captivating outlier in chemical dynamics.

Water - An Unusual Hydrogen Bond

The internal vibration which water molecules have is not the only anomaly of water's molecular chemistry. The next surprising fact is all about interaction between water molecules. They are always interacting with and attracting each other. Water molecules are electrically neutral. It is balanced. However, the charges are not uniformly distributed. There is a separation of the positive and negative charges. It is because of two facts. First is the arrangement around the oxygen and the second is the presence of lone pair electrons.

The lone pair electrons are not involved in the covalent bonds and are left alone. These lone pairs are very negative as they contain two negative electrons each. These repulsive forces act to push the hydrogen closer to the electrons on the oxygen. The bend angle structure of 104.5° plays an important role here.

The bent structure of water provides water with two distinct "sides": one side of the water molecule has two negative lone pairs, while the other side presents the two hydrogens. The hydrogen side is positive. They get this way because of the "electronegativity" of oxygen.

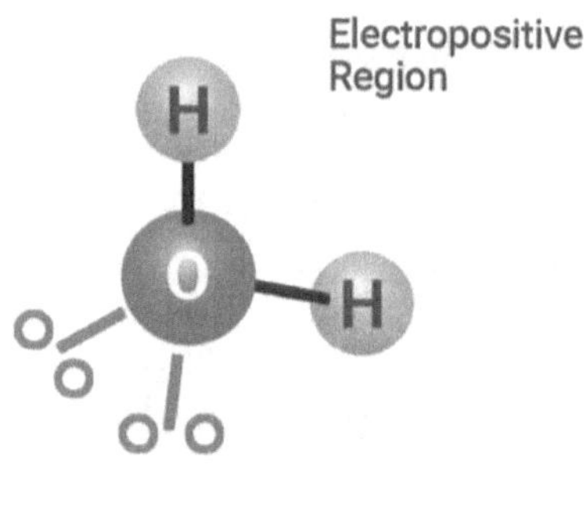

Fig-17 Water with two distinct sides

Electronegativity is a measure of how much one atom wants to have electrons. Oxygen wants to have electrons more than hydrogen does. Because of this difference in electronegativity, the electrons in the covalent bonds between oxygen and hydrogen get pulled slightly toward the oxygen.

This leaves the hydrogen a little bit electron-deficient and thus slightly positive. Because of this, water has a slightly negative and a positive end. It can also interact with itself and form a highly organized 'inter-molecular' network. The positive hydrogen end of one molecule can interact favourably with the negative lone pair of another water molecule. This interaction is called "Hydrogen Bonding".

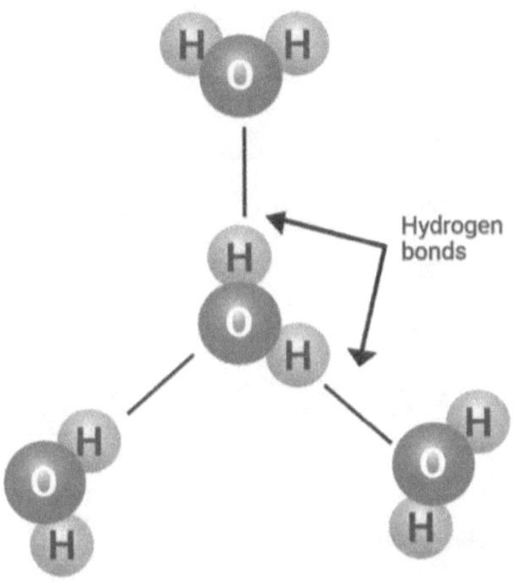

Fig-18 Hydrogen bonding

Every one of the water molecules can form four hydrogen bonds, and thus, an elaborate network of molecules is formed. That's why water is not just a simple liquid. It's a network of interacting molecules held together by these special hydrogen bonds. This polar arrangement of oxygen and hydrogen allows the water molecules to become attracted to many other different types of molecules. Water also has a very high viscosity due to this hydrogen bonding.

Hydrogen bonds are always in a rearrangement as their networks are distorted and floppier. A normal liquid water structure contains five molecules. However, in ice, it is a ring of six molecules. In certain situations, it can be of four molecules due to the distorted and dancing nature of the hydrogen bond.

The ice matrix has the same symmetry as a hexagon, and it contains a lot of space. In any solid materials, molecules are packed densely due to the attractive interaction between them. Solid materials will exhibit only two or three structures at different pressures, but ice can have about 12 structures when it is squeezed.

Water and the Diploe Moment

Surface tension, capillary action, and the fourth phase of water are already discussed previously. However, regarding the surface tension, there are other findings. Mercury has the highest surface tension as we know it today. But it is an elemental liquid. Water has the highest surface tension of all compounds. But how does water get this high surface tension property?

The scientific explanation for this is the dipole moment of water. The dipole moment is the measurement of the separation of two opposite electrical charges. This dipole moment will arise when a chemical bond between two atoms of different electronegativity occurs. This movement of electrons represents the dipole moment. The larger the electronegativity difference between the two atoms, the larger the bond's dipole moment and polarity.

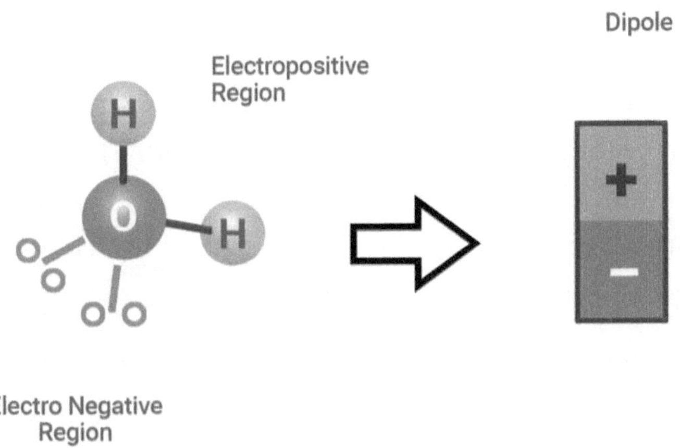

Fig-19 Dipole Moment of water

Water has unique and permanent dipole moments due to the presence of lone pair electrons. This is a unique anomaly as many symmetrical molecules do not have permanent dipole moments. Dipole moments lead to strong intermolecular interactions within themselves and lead to high surface tension.

Water and Heat Things

Water boils at an extremely high temperature because of the extensive network of Hydrogen bonds in it. The Hydrogen bonds are cohesive forces, and they hold the water molecules together. The process of boiling requires a lot more energy due to this. The freezing point of the water also is much higher because of the hydrogen bonding.

The formation of water from hydrogen and oxygen not only produces water but also a substantial amount of energy, approximately 572 kJ (Kilojoule). This phenomenon is called exothermic reaction, which means it generates energy. This is also an example of combustion reaction. This significant release of energy is the main reason why scientists are exploring hydrogen fuel. It is a green fuel without any harmful residue as water is the only product.

The remarkable anomaly of water's high specific heat plays a crucial role in sustaining life on Earth. Unlike similar compounds, water exhibits an exceptional capacity to absorb and retain heat. Water can absorb five times more heat than sand and ten times more than iron.

The oceans, lakes and other water bodies help regulate temperatures that people experience. Water absorbs the heat during the day and is released at night. Cities near water bodies take a longer time to heat up and a longer time to cool down than the rest of the land. Hence, places near the oceans will tend to have less change in temperatures than inland cities. In some instances, even frozen lakes and bodies of water resist complete melting during the summer months, showcasing nature's innate mechanism for temperature control through the extraordinary properties of water.

Water has an exceptionally high specific heat capacity. Raising of water temperature requires a lot of heat energy. At sea level, water boils at 100°C. But at Mount Everest, we can boil the water at 68°C. This change in boiling point is due to the relationship between atmospheric pressure and vapour pressure of water. Boiling happens when the vapour pressure of water exceeds the atmospheric pressure. At higher altitudes, atmospheric pressure is lower, and it makes water molecules break their bonds. The higher the altitude, lower the boiling point of water.

Water at boiling temperature is not the same as boiling water. When water first reaches boiling, it does not begin to turn to steam. More energy is needed to begin turning the boiling liquid water into gaseous water vapours. The bonds holding water molecules as a liquid are not easily broken. Water's compressibility drops once the temperature increases beyond 46 degrees Celsius, whereas, for most liquids, the compressibility is directly proportional to the temperature. Also, most liquids become viscous when the temperature rises but water becomes less viscous at high temperatures.

Supercritical Fluid

Water has an unusually high critical point. Water behaves uniquely at its critical point, a temperature of 374 °C and a pressure of 217 atmospheres. Water is a supercritical fluid above this temperature. Supercritical means a highly compressed state having the properties of liquid and gas. At this stage, water can diffuse through solids just like a gas but also dissolve things just like a liquid. It is also known as the "fourth state of water".

Supercooled Water

"Supercooled water" is a fascinating behaviour of water often observed in clouds, raindrops, and frigid environments. Supercooled water refers to a state where water is in a liquid state well below its usual freezing temperature of 0°C. The presence of impurities in the water acts as nucleation sites for water which facilitates the crystallisation process. When water is pure, it can stay well below the freezing point.

The dissolved substances like salt can also lower the freezing point of water. That's why salt is often spread on the road to prevent ice formation. In the Antarctic Ocean, the higher salt concentration results in a lower freezing point and the water is supercooled. However, blood will freeze at this temperature making our survival difficult in these regions. Supercooled water can be found at temperatures as low as -60 °C.

Water Density Play

The water density is more complicated as we discussed earlier. Water expands upon freezing. Other liquids contract and sink. Water is most dense at 4° Celsius but becomes lighter when the temperature is below this point. This anomaly of water saves marine life in winter. Hydrogen bonding is one of the reasons for this behaviour. Depending on temperature variations, water molecules undergo structural rearrangements, leading to an expansion of the substance and a decrease in density.

This dynamic restructuring is not a singular event, but rather a continuous process, occurring multiple times in response to diverse temperature and pressure conditions. In a recent scientific investigation involving the exposure of water to different pressures and temperatures, researchers discovered that water exhibited 17 distinct structural arrangements as it continuously adapted to its environment.

The density of water varies with the amount of material that is dissolved in it. Major dissolved contents in the natural water are minerals, gases, and salts. Density will increase when more and more materials are dissolved in water.

Seawater is denser than pure water due to this reason. But here also, nature adopted a system to its advantage. Because of the high density of the seawater, sound can travel longer distances. Sound has a velocity of 1545 meters/second in seawater at 30°C, which is about 3,500 miles per hour. This means sound can travel four times faster than through air. Many marine mammals like whales and dolphins have used this communication method that can be heard over vast oceanic expanses.

Water and Soil

The weird behaviour of water is a blessing to our planet. As we know, plants get nutrients from the soil. But how the soil is formed?

They are formed mainly due to the erosion of rocks caused by water. The high surface tension of water with its capability of expansion in freezing results in the erosion of rocks. Hence, soil is produced. Further interaction of water with chemicals, bacteria and a variety of other geographical influences make the soil rich in nutrients. The survival of vegetation happens only due to these collaborative efforts.

Water - The Insulator

Water has a high "dielectric constant" property. This property makes water a universal solvent. Dielectric means an ability to store electrical charges but shows very low electrical conductivity. This is the reason pure water is an insulator and does not conduct electricity.

The complexities of water's structure, interactions, and bonding mechanisms exert a deep influence on our daily lives and surroundings. Nature cleverly harnesses the unique characteristics of water to its advantage, coordinating unusual behaviours that sustain life on Earth.

Water, in its molecular complexities, plays a vital role in shaping our existence. However, the sophisticated dance between the anomalies of water and the effect of geological processes is not fully understood, leaving us with a significant knowledge gap.

Water is a complex and dynamic entity that harbours many mysteries waiting to be unravelled. Although we have made remarkable advancements in science and technology, many questions regarding water remain unanswered. The origin of water on Earth itself is a fascinating and complex mystery that has puzzled everyone.

Understanding the origin of water is crucial to resolving the mysteries of our planet's early history and the conditions that allowed life to emerge. Several theories have been proposed to explain the origin of water. However, none can be definitively proven enough to contribute to our evolving understanding of this essential element. The mystery is still lying with water as we know only 5% of our planet. With each new revelation, we may come closer to water's past, present, and future.

Chapter 7

Water – An Alien Substance

*"A drop of water, if it could write out its
own history, would explain the universe to us."*

– *Lucy Larcom*

The opening chapter of the Bible begins with, "God created heaven and earth". As per the Bible, there was no Earth, sky, humans, or animals in the beginning. The universe was created in six days. God created light on the first day, and earth and water on the second day. On the third day, he separated water and land, made the sea, and covered the land with plants and trees. He created the Sun, Moon, and stars on the fourth day and other living creatures like fish and birds on the fifth day. Finally, on the sixth day, he created man along with other creatures and the creation was completed.

As per Islam, Allah created the universe. He made all living and non-living creatures, planets, water and so on. The creation took six days, and you can see many similarities in the creation process in the Abrahamic faiths - Christianity, Judaism, and Islam

In Greek mythology, the story starts with emptiness. Within the emptiness, *Gaea*, the Goddess of Earth emerges. She gives birth to her son Uranus. *Gaea* and Uranus together produce the population of titans, humans, monsters etc.

The ancient Mesopotamian creation story is entirely different. There was water in the beginning. *Apsu* (sweet water) and *Tiamat* (saltwater) - one male and the other female. From their union, monsters and gods were created. The female creator, *Tiamat* wants to take control, but her descendants unite against her and kill her. The corpse of *Tiamat* was pierced into two. With half, the heaven, and with the other half, the Earth was created. They killed her evil partner *Kungu* and with his blood, the first human was created.

In the Chinese folklore, the creation *Pan Ku* hatched from a cosmic egg. One half of the shell became the sky, and the other half became Earth. They started growing for years until they fell into pieces. *Pan Ku*'s limbs became mountains, his blood became rivers, his breath became wind, his voice became thunder, his eyes became Sun and Moon, and his body became manhood.

Most religions in the world have one thing in common. They believe that God is the creator of water. I will explain many civilisational aspects of water in later chapters. Before that, we will uncover the ongoing research and debate within the scientific community about the origin of water. Discoveries are developing in each decade and continue to refine our understanding. Let me narrate the scientific findings on the origin of water.

Whenever we talk about the origin of water, I get overwhelmed just like you. There are so many theories, findings, and arguments that if you were to Google, every finding would have its contradictions. But to believe in something we have to start somewhere, right? As far as we know, the beginning of Earth was something like this.

A proton is a very tiny and extremely small part of an atom. It is so small that even an infinitesimal dot made from a pen can contain 500 billion of them. About 13.80 billion years ago, one day, protons collided with each other and started joining together in a matter of seconds. It then started expanding and filling. With this limitless expansion, matter formed. It had no dimensions, no space, no past, no present, and no reference points. The universe emerged from nothingness. It then started expanding, and within a timeframe, most of the matter was produced, including our universe. That's what we believe, scientifically speaking. But what caused this "Big Bang" moment is still a mystery as we still don't what existed before or what triggered the explosion.

When the universe was formed, it was extremely hot - more than 10 billion degrees Celsius. Some kind of action or nuclear reaction began that aided in creating our atmosphere and elements. The first elements were hydrogen and helium.

The Sun was surrounded by a hot gaseous disc with a mixture of all types of atoms. As a result of varied kinds of actions and reactions for many centuries, the gaseous disc cooled down. Many elements and compounds started forming our universe and its planets. These larger molecules started sticking together and forming clusters of dust and particles. The dust particles and clumps collided with each other to become large and began to attract each other due to due gravity. Many planets, sub-planets, and asteroids were formed this way. One of which happens to be our solar system and the formation of our planet Earth.

The solar system too was very hot. However, the ideal position of the Earth from the Sun and the positioning of the Moon allowed the Earth to cool. The sweet spot in our solar system where the Earth resides is called the Goldilocks Zone. In this zone, a planet's surface temperature is neither too hot nor too cold. Oxygen, an element which is formed in our atmosphere condensed with several other elements including Hydrogen and Helium.

The Earth began releasing various types of gases from its surface. Sooner or later, the earth got an atmosphere. When an ideal situation of the temperature and pressure occurred, hydrogen and oxygen atoms bonded together. The radiation of the sun energised the oxygen and hydrogen atoms floating in the atmosphere. They crashed into each other, and water was born this way. When the Earth was further cooled, the water vapour from the atmosphere condensed out and rained back. It rained for many centuries and liquid water was stored on the Earth. It is estimated that this phenomenon happened almost four billion years ago. That is the age of water on Earth.

The above-said happenings are the most convincing finding of the origin of Earth and water. But it does not end here, and some contradictory findings came up. The second type of scientific explanation is related to comets and asteroids. Over centuries, the comets and asteroids positioned at a higher distance from Earth were cooled and condensed into ice. Some of these comets and asteroids collided while they were passing through the Earth's orbit. Water formed on the surface of the Earth as a result of the bombardment of these wet comets and asteroids.

Halley's Comet, the most famous comet in our history, offers valuable insights into the theory of comet and asteroid bombardment. This comet makes a reappearance in Earth's vicinity approximately once every 76 years. Its most recent appearance was in 1986, and it is expected to return in 2061. In 1986, several spacecraft managed to fly past the comet, taking close-up pictures of its nucleus. The images revealed that the comet is 15 by 8 kilometres in size and its nucleus is made up of a mixture of water, volatile gases, and mineral dust.

Earth is the only planet in our solar system with a huge amount of water. Water covers 70.8% of the Earth's surface and it is estimated to be 1.38 to 1.50 billion cubic kilometres. This is only an estimate as we are yet to fathom the exact depth of oceans at various locations. Apart from this, the scientific community is trying to find out the quantity of water stored in Earth's bowels. It is assumed that bowel water can fill the oceans many times. Some scientists believe that it is impossible to create this huge reservoir of water through a comet or asteroid bombardment.

This brings us to the third finding.

When the solar system was formed, most of the planets including the Earth had a ring around them. These rings were formed around the equator of the sun and converted into planets due to the push-pull force. These rings are believed to be water-ice.

The ring around the Earth was sandwiched between Earth and the Moon. Earth was pulling the ring inward, and the Moon was pulling it outwards for a long period. However, the ring was stationary at its position.

For the unversed, it should be noted that the Moon is inching away from Earth at the rate of 3.8 cm per year. Due to this reverse movement of the moon for centuries, the pulling force of the Moon reduced gradually, and the water-ice rings collapsed into the Earth. The ring melted with friction and water formed and was stored in the Earth.

The water spread to the north and south directions from the equator and formed oceans. This theory suggests that the ocean formed on Earth almost 1 billion years ago which is much later than its creation. If you calculate the Moon's receding with time and distance based on this theory, it makes some sense to believe this phenomenon too.

Secondly, you can still find rings on some planets in the solar system including Saturn and Jupiter. The composition of rings on these two celestial bodies is believed to be of, again, water–ice.

The fourth theory proposes that, around 4.5 billion years ago, Earth collided with a planetesimal, about the size of Mars. This theory is similar to the theory of bombardment of comets and asteroids. The impact of this collision was tremendous, and the Earth was left with a ball of molten rock called magma. Many scientists believe that this collusion played a crucial role in the formation of the Moon.

When the Earth condensed after millions of years, water and other substances like carbon dioxide are condensed. This process eventually gave an atmosphere and water bodies to Earth. The validation of this theory was backed by the planetary scientists who studied the meteorites. These studies found that many meteorites contain water ice, ammonia, carbon dioxide, minerals, and other volatile components.

The above findings are the scientific hypothesis of the origin of water on Earth. Many of you might have read different theories too. Whatever may be the viewpoint of the origin of water on Earth, the mystery keeps going deeper when we talk about our planet's ability to hold water.

The bombardment, clashes of oxygen and hydrogen etc. happened not only on Earth alone but on many planets, but these planets were not able to store water in them. Various studies and pictures from the satellite show that Mars once upon a time had water which eventually dried out. So, what makes Earth such a special place to be gifted with water? Is it the positioning of Earth in the solar system, or its atmosphere, or something else?

Still, the experiment on the Big Bang is under various stages and developments; we may get some contradictory revelations about today's understanding in later years. However, we are still in the dark, and therefore, can neither conclude nor confirm one single and most comprehensive fact about the origin of water. Over the years, we may have a more credible and constructive answer.

The mystery of the origin of water on Earth is a complex and exciting puzzle. Based on multiple hypotheses, water comes to earth from somewhere else. It is extraterrestrial.

When our understanding of planetary formation and the solar system's history develops further, we may be able to solve the remaining mysteries surrounding the presence of water here.

As for the origin of water, life in it is also a mistrial topic where many theories have evolved. The fundamental role water plays in the emergence and sustenance of life is still a mystery. Let's find out.

Chapter 8

Water: The creator of Life

"If there is magic on this planet,
it is contained in water."

– Loren Eiseley

As per Hinduism, life originated in water. The first life creation was a fish-like creature called *Matsya*. It is known as the first *avatar* (incarnation) of Lord Vishnu. The second *avatar* was *Kurma*, a tortoise, indicating the oviparous nature of the reproduction of offspring. The third one was *Varaha*, the boar indicating the mammal nature of reproduction. The fourth one was *Narasimha*, a half-man, and half-animal, then *Vamana*, a dwarf, a small man and from their various *avatars* based on the evolutionary and intellectual process described.

When water was available on Earth, the planet used to be very hot. Once the atmosphere was stabilised, the Earth had an internal structure. Heavy elements like metals were pressed to the centre of the Earth and water rose to the surface. The heated water from inside the Earth vapourised into the atmosphere. The carbon dioxide level started falling, the atmospheric pressure and temperature dropped, and vapourised water condensed and rained back on the Earth's surface. The air aided this process and then the extraordinary phenomenon began – the temperature started dropping.

About 3.8 to 4.1 million years ago, a set of molecules ascended. These molecules merged in water and formed long-chain polymers. Scientists believe that RNA (ribonucleic acid) was one of the first biological molecules present in the water. After RNA, the DNA (Deoxyribonucleic acid) and protein molecules formed. These three molecules are essential for the formation of life. The first part of the genetic ingredient could have been made this way. However, we are still not able to succeed in recreating the first RNA molecules formed in the water, emphasising the mystic nature of water.

The molecules started replicating naturally based on the surrounding conditions. The Earth's atmosphere and water provided favourable surroundings. Over a period, simple molecules developed into larger, more complex biological molecules and then into cells. Following further diversification, some cells are metabolically capable of the photosynthesis process, and therefore, the biological and geochemical cycles started.

As per Charles Darwin's theory of evolution, life started in a warm little pond. This pond consisted of several kinds of ammonia, salts, lights, heat, etc. The cellular microorganism underwent many complex changes due to this, and the living presence occurred. This evolution was a natural process that produced more offspring leading to different rates of survival and reproduction.

These offspring adapted and survived in varying situations. This survival and development took place according to the environment and conditions which caused evolution. Evolution and life emerged through a complex chain of events based on natural law, dictated by the physical-chemical environment of Earth and water. Evolutionary processes gave rise to diversity at every level of biological organisation.

During the process of evolution, aquatic vegetal life developed and released oxygen into the atmosphere. Then ozone gas appeared and started building up. This ozone absorbed harmful ultraviolet radiations which resulted in life on Earth.

The cellular microorganisms which appeared in the water floated and moved due to buoyancy. Oxygen supported the biological development and diversification of the early microorganisms. The ozone served as a blanket protecting and filtering harmful UV radiation. These dramatic changes transformed early Earth into our present-day biosphere.

The assembling of the first cellular life happened on the Earth in the presence of three essential substances: water, energy, and organic compounds. Centuries of evolution finally gave the Earth its most perfect creation – homo sapiens.

Apart from the theory of evolution, several theories are afloat regarding the origin of life. Theories range from life beginning from deep-sea thermal vents to extraterrestrial bacteria appearing from different places in the universe. Recently, there are more versions of life on Earth. Some theories claim that life did not originate here, but it reached from the inside of a meteor that hit the Earth.

But there is another aspect which we neglect today. The form of life from non-living matters to living matters started with Greek philosophy. This is based on heterogeneity. Heterogeneous is the process of derivation of one form of life transmuted to another form of life. One type of animal can descend from another type of animal. This deriving process made a different set of living things such as flies from putrid matter, mice from dirty grass, crocodiles from rotting logs and so on. This is considered a spontaneous generation. Aristotle was believed to endorse the same philosophy and it was approved by the world till evolution theory was established.

One thing that arises beyond doubt is the fact that life began in water.

The anomalies of water played a major role in the Earth's history. The memory of water, high surface tension and capillary action, crooked geometric shape and weird angle, the fourth phase, interaction between water molecules, hydrogen bonding, dipole moments, dielectric constant, high specific heat, density, high surface tension, and other anomalies explained in various chapters breaches the basic physio-chemical understanding and question all principles and theories of a normal liquid function.

Yet, in many of the world's most scientific and complex laboratories, water and its properties are still tested till date. Maybe in the future, we will have the right kind of technology and a more acceptable mindset to understand water as a whole and put an end to all doubts. Until then, water will have the last laugh while we still try to decode its magic!

My intention in writing this book is not to get into a scientific debate, but to get a conscious awareness about water and tell how it can benefit us beyond hydration or quenching our thirst. I leave the science to your judgment.

Now, I'll take you through religious perspectives of water in the next chapters.

Chapter 9

Countless Religions, Counting on Water

"It is the waters that pervade everything, big or small, the earth, the atmosphere, the heaven, the mountains, gods, men, animals, birds, grass, plants, dogs, worms, insects, ants… All these (worldly manifestations) are waters indeed. They are the foundations of all in the universe".

— Chhandogya Upanishad – 7.10.1

In my childhood, most nights I would fall asleep listening to mythological stories. *Ummi Amma* and *Radhamma* were good storytellers, and they narrated many treasure troves of stories from Hindu mythology to put me to sleep. When I started my research about water, my familiar territory was mythology. I was curious to know the activities performed by *Ummi Amma* & *Radhamma* during my illness. I decided to delve into mythology first and look into the religions, tribes, and their understanding of water. It was amazing.

Ancient civilisations harboured a shared conviction: the elemental source of life manifests itself within the aqueous realms.

This collective belief, though initially steeped in myth and mysticism, aligns remarkably with contemporary scientific insights. The significance of water in the context of life is not a cultural artefact. It bridges the gap between ancient wisdom and modern understanding. The connection between life and water is not arbitrary. It aligns with the fundamental properties of water.

If you go through the journey of every civilisation and religion, irrespective of where it originated, every culture considers water to be special. Water was God. Water plays a vital role in everybody's life as a saviour, destroyer, protector, and messenger.

Irrespective of our educational and socio-economic backgrounds, most of us believe in one thing, the existence of God. We may have different religions, castes, creeds, races, and different ways of worshipping, but everything narrows down to one common thing - the God factor!

As per sociologist Ariela Keyser and Juhum Navarro-Rivera's review of atheism, 7% of the world population are atheists and agnostics. If this is right, then 93% of the world population today believe in some or the other form of God. As the official motto written in an American dollar "In God, we trust".

Before I begin to explain, let me clarify that certain facts and findings that I am going to state here are only for signifying the importance of water. It is my observation, and I am neither endorsing nor rejecting any belief system. I respect all religions alike, and I believe in all. My parents' religion and caste which I inherited have nothing to do with this book or my findings.

We don't know for sure when the first human was born. Scientifically it has been suggested that we, as human beings, have existed on Earth for more than 300,000 years. What were our ancestors doing for so many centuries? We don't know.

Our existence for so many years is not known to us. No history for countless millennia. Our ancestors who stayed in the forests moved out, discovered fire, ate cooked food, started staying together as groups, made homes, and finally, the so-called civilisation came into existence. Rules and regulations were formulated, habitats were formed and finally, civilisations transformed based on belief systems.

Ancient history mainly talks about four civilisations. Egyptians, Indus, Mesopotamians, and Mayans. We don't know when it started. We are still digging to find out. We have history only of the past 10,000 years. This essentially means we don't have any clue about the belief system before that period.

As far as the documented history is concerned, Hinduism, Zoroastrianism, and Judaism are the oldest and largest belief systems created by human beings which continue to exist even today. The same is true of Taoism and Confucianism. Other belief systems include Egyptians, Romans, Greeks, Mayans, Native Americans etc. but most are near extinction or are today being practised by limited people in a particular geography. Next comes Buddhism and Jainism, then Christianity from where BC ends, AD starts, then Islam, followed by many other religions.

The belief system for the ancient religions is in such a way that I have dedicated exclusive chapters for some of the largest existing religions. Each one will be analysed with its own perspective. It is up to you to read all or just the tradition you believe in. In the end, you will find what you are seeking. All belief systems work similarly, but at the same time, differently!

Water – The Divine Mother

"Aapo Hi Sstthaa Mayo-Bhuvasthaa
Na Uurje Dadhaatana

Mahe Rannaatha Cakssase

Tasmaa Aram Gamaama Vo Yasya Kssayaaya Jinvatha

Aapo Janayathaa Ca Nah

"O Water, because of your presence, the Atmosphere is so
refreshing and imparts us with vigour and strength.
We revere you who gladdens us by your Pure essence.

O Water, when your invigorating essence goes to
one affected by weakness, it enlivens him,

O Water, you are the source of our lives."

– Apah Suktam

Indus Valley Civilisation is one of the oldest civilisations that existed on the Earth. Originating and spread across the Indian sub-continent, the Indus Valley Civilisation was the foundational ethos, of diverse belief systems such as Jainism, Buddhism, Shaivism, Vaishnavism, and Shaktism. Over time, Shaivism, Vaishnavism, and Shaktism gradually converged, adopting a shared acceptance that ultimately merged into what is now widely recognized as "Hinduism".

Initially, the word Hindu (deriving from the word Sindhu or Indus, the river) was only a geographical identification given by travellers to the Indus Valley, basically traders from other parts of the world. The geography between the Himalayas and the Indian Ocean was known as Indus or *Indoi* in Greek and later called Hindus. Throughout millennia, this civilisation went through various distinctive transformations, migrations, interculturalism, vanquishing, invasion etc. which influenced and changed the perceptions in many areas. The outsider's term Hindus slowly became used by its people to separate them from others. Slowly, the ethnicity, culture and geographical identification converted into a religious perspective. The term "Hinduism" is very new and used only since the 19th century by the Britishers who colonised the Indian subcontinent. Today, Hinduism is commonly known as the Vedic religion with a polytheistic belief system.

The first reference to God in Hinduism is given in the four Vedas. Vedas are the pillars of their belief systems. The original Vedas are very fluid in nature. In its text, it has constant references to *bhoodevi* (Mother Earth) and includes all five elements along with its extensive flora and fauna. Not surprisingly, in the Vedas, water is considered divine.

In this belief system, *Brahman* is the ultimate and unchanging reality. It is within and beyond the world. In the Sanskrit language, *Brahman* has been described as the highest reality - *Sachidananda* which can be broken down as *Sat-Chit-Ananda* (being-consciousness-bliss).

Brahman, the ultimate essence, is a gender-neutral concept and is referred to as the supreme self. It is the universal substrate from which all material things originate and return after their dissolution. Its numerous forms signify the true essence of *Brahman* and the true source of life. In short, all reality has its source in *Brahman*.

In Hinduism, water is identified with *Brahman*. In the Vedic creation theory, time was the first manifestation followed by *Aham*, representing materials knowledge, activities, and ingredients. The next step was the creation of basic elements including fire, air, water, and ether (sky), followed by Earth. Thereafter, the process of creation is continued with many manifestations. The origin of water specified in the Rig Veda can be loosely translated as follows.

> *"Darkness was hidden by darkness in the*
> *beginning, with no*
> *distinguishing sign, all this was water.*
> *The life force that was covered with emptiness,*
> *that One arose through the power of heat.*
> *Desire came upon that One in the beginning,*
> *that was the first seed of mind".*

> — Rig Veda 10: 129

Apart from four major Vedas, a multitude of supplementary Vedas, Upanishads, and Puranas emerged, collectively from the fabric of Hinduism. In all these sacred scriptures, water is recognised as the prerequisite for the creation and sustenance of life on Earth.

Water, considered an extra-terrestrial thing, originated beyond Earth, and not only laid the foundation of life but also actively participated in the life process of both living and non-living on Earth. The below verse underscores the profound significance of water.

> *"apo va idaṃ sarvaṃ visva bhutanyapaḥ*
> *praṇa va apaḥ pasava*
> *apo'nnamapo'mṛtamapaḥ samraḍapo viraḍapaḥ*
> *svaraḍapaschandaṃsyapo*
> *jyotiṃsyapo yajuṃsyapaḥ satyamapaḥ sarva devata*
> *apo bhurbhuvaḥ suvarapa om"*
> *"Verily all this is water. All the created beings are water.*
> *The vital breath in the body*
> *is water. Quadrupeds are water. Edible crops are water.*
> *Ambrosia is water. Samraṭ is*
> *water. Viraṭ is water. Svaraṭ is water. The metres are*
> *water. The luminar Vedic formulas are water. Truth is*
> *water. All deities are water. The three worlds denoted by*
> *Bhuḥ, Bhuvaḥ and Suvaḥ are water. The source of all*
> *these is the supreme, denoted by the syllable om".*
>
> *– Mahanarayaṇa Upaniṣad*

Punyam Aham

In the Hindu belief system, there are many gods, but majorly renowned in three categories. *Brahmanda Devata* (Universal God), *Kula Devata* (God of Profession & Clan), *Grama Devata* (Village God). Apart from this, the belief system provides the ultimate freedom to choose a personal god (*Ishta Devata*).

Temples are made not only for worship but also to take care of the physical, emotional, and spiritual well-being. Each temple, especially the old ones, is made with the consecration of a particular energy form and the deity is placed at the centre of the temple. A deity is considered a living form with a specified consecrated energy source of a particular god or goddess.

Various rituals, offerings, and prayers are offered to the deity every day, and strict, customised, and sophisticated patterns are followed each day. Most of the deities of the temples are made of special stone, metal alloy, and rarely, special wood. An elaborate process is involved from the very beginning of making the idol to its consecration.

In many such temples, water is used in a variety of offerings and plays a very vital role in the temple proceedings. One of the important rituals involved with water is *"punyaham" which* loosely translates to a sacred day or blessed time. It can also translate as knowing the meaning of two Sanskrit words *punya* and *aham*. *Punya* has many meanings including saintly, sacred, good, pure etc. and *aham* means self, so *Punya Aham* is self-purification or acquiring saintly nature or good qualities.

Punyaham is performed before most of the important rituals and is carried out to eliminate impurities. A mantra is often chanted during the *punyaham* process. Mantra is a sacred utterance believed to have magical and spiritual powers. *Punyaaham* is the sacred thing to be received while praying. Mantras are repeated several times on the water which is received by the devotees as *punyaham.* Devotees consume and sprinkle this holy water.

The Hindu belief system has recognised the power of memory, energy, and the various other dimensions of the water. *Punyaham* is the best example of the same. The *punyaham* is believed to carry the memories of the mantra chanting along with the positive energies of the place. These memories and positive energies can enter the human body through consumption and sprinkling. It is believed that through *punyaaham,* the mind and body get cleansed and awakened, and through the power of the awakened mind, all human beings can achieve success. Moreover, this ritual is said to be highly effective leading to the attainment of an aura of action, purity of words, long life, happiness and so on.

Mantra Snanam – The Chanting Bath

As per Hinduism, water purifies the body and mind, and rejuvenates the soul. Hinduism believes in cycles of birth and death. The fundamental idea of every Hindu is to attain moksha, liberation from the birth cycle, and dissolving with *Brahma*n.

Every birth is the journey to reach this goal. Hindus believe that water nourishes and sustains the spirit (soul) and the body. If the water is used in a certain way, they believe it can also erase the bad karma from the past life. The idea of *mantra snanam* is all about this.

Mantra is a sacred utterance and *snanam* means bath. Various books and writings in Hinduism extolled the therapeutic, spiritual, and divine power of water. It is believed that for one who performs *mantasnanam* regularly, the water will sanctify their spiritual aspiration and uplift the individual from the mundane to the transcendental.

Hindus engage in the ritual of *mantrasnanam* as a regular practice, carefully chosen to align with the surrounding topography. This sacred act involves cleansing oneself in various natural water sources such as streams, rivers, ponds, lakes, waterfalls, and even during rainfall.

Before the commencement of *mantrasnanam,* they cup water in both hands or with their right hand, reciting sacred mantras into it. Subsequently, they ceremoniously spread the water around themselves, creating a symbolic boundary of sanctity. The final step involves immersing oneself in the water, establishing a profound connection between the spiritual verses, and the sacred water.

Fig-20 Mantrasnanam (Prayer and bath in water)

River Goddesses

Hindus often offer *aarti*, (worship with a lighting lamp) with prayers to rivers and water bodies which symbolises the relation between fire and water. In Hinduism, water stands for purification, rejuvenation, prosperity, and male-female unity. Fire stands for bonding and purity. Water and fire are considered purifiers due to their applicability and higher detergency.

As per Hinduism, major rivers like Ganga (Ganges), Yamuna, Saraswathi, Narmada, Kaveri, Sindhu, and Godavari are worshipped as seven sacred rivers and considered goddesses. It is every religious Hindu's life aspiration to take a holy dip in all these rivers in their lifetime. This pilgrimage is called *"Teerth yatra"*.

Varanasi, situated on the banks of the Ganga, is considered one of the oldest inhabited cities in the world and a major pilgrimage site. It is believed that dying in Varanasi and being cremated along the Ganga can lead to liberation from the cycle of rebirth.

Ganga is considered one of the holiest rivers in Hinduism. Its water is believed to possess purifying and spiritually rejuvenating properties. The holy river is revered as Goddess Ganga, and her water is referred to as *Gangajal*. It is believed that *Gangajal* is self-cleansing in nature and a single dip in it will wash away all the sins of a person. The ritual act of taking *Gangaja*l home is a common practice among Hindus, who utilize it to cleanse not only their residences but also the local water resources.

Ganga River possesses a distinctive ability to maintain its freshness over an extended period, presenting a great mystery that has fascinated scientists for centuries. D.S. Bhargava, a famous Indian environmental engineer, and professor of hydrology has devoted a lifetime to unravelling the extraordinary properties of Ganga.

In an exhaustive three-year study, Bhargava thoroughly measured the river's remarkable self-cleansing prowess. Ganga can reduce its biochemical oxygen demand (BOD) levels much faster than other rivers. According to Bhargava, Ganga exhibits a self-purifying quality that results in high oxygen levels - a staggering 25 times higher than any other river worldwide. The river expeditiously eliminates suspended wastes 15 to 20 times faster when compared to other rivers.

A recent study found that bacteriophage - a virus having the capacity to consume bacteria - gives an antibacterial characteristic to the waters of Ganga. This high bacteriophage load imparts a mystical quality to its waters. Some scientists are actively engaged in sediment experiments and a meticulous study of sediment surface chemistry. They hope this study can provide scientific validation for the mysterious potency of *Gangajal*.

The *Maha Kumbh Mela*, also known as the "Festival of the Sacred Pitcher", stands as an extraordinary pilgrimage that unfolds once every 12 years. This is the marking of a profound convergence of spirituality, devotion, and tradition of Hinduism. It is the largest congregation of pilgrims in the world. This magnificent spectacle occurs at four riverbank sites: Prayagraj and Haridwar, both located along the river Ganga; Nasik, gracing the banks of the river Godavari; and Ujjain, situated on the shores of the river Shipra. This sacred gathering lies in the transformative act of taking a dip in the waters of these revered rivers. This symbolic immersion is deeply ingrained in the belief that it cleanses the soul of impurities and sins, providing a sacred rebirth and accompanying a renewed journey along the spiritual path.

All major rivers, except *Brahmaputra,* named in Hinduism have feminine names which show their beauty and motherly qualities. It is significant enough to note that the Hindu belief system promotes the theory that life begins in the water. The orderly manner in the *Dashavatar* (the 10 *avatars* of Lord

Vishnu) described in the Hindu texts resembles the origin of life in the water and human evolutionary theory.

Water Vedas

The four Vedas illustrate the presence of divinity of five elements called *Pancha bhootha*. *Agni* (Fire), *Vayu* (Air), *Tapas* (Water), *Prithvi* (Earth) and *Akash* (Space) are the five great elements. *Mitra* (Sun God), *Agni* (fire god), Vayu (God of Air), Varuna (The god of the ocean), and *Indra* (the king of Gods and God of Rain, and thunder) are the foremost Gods described in Vedas. Each signifies these elements.

If we examine the hymns of the Vedas, the relationship between water and humans is very well documented. As per the Vedas, at the formation of the world, water was subsequent to none. The people could not think of another proceedings substance from which water was derived. Hence, water was given a unique significance. The Vedas say water prevents and eliminates all diseases. Furthermore, any type of medicine can be found in the water.

There are several divine forces prominently associated with water in Vedas. Indra is given importance more than other gods and is considered the God of Gods. Indra is the god of rain and thunderstorms, and he possesses *vajrayudha,* a lightning thunderbolt weapon. Indra rescuing waters for sustaining life on the earth is described in hundreds of hymns in the Rig Veda. Vedic people perform rituals to Indra when they are in desperate need of rain.

Varuna, the god of the ocean, has a unique place in the Vedas. He is the regulator of water that causes the rivers to flow and move waters. Varuna is the most frightful god as he maintains a cosmic order and he is prayed for forgiveness of any sinful acts done by the people.

Rig Veda's views on the origin of water are recognised beyond the deed of human capacity. In Rig Veda, water is credited with motherhood. She is often found being begged for strength, protection and longevity while looking after one's health in his household.

In Atharva Veda, it is written that the great sage Vishwakarma placed a seed in the cosmic waters to create the earth and the sky. Atharva Veda is replete with medicinal hymns and many hymns are about using water to cure several internal diseases and discomforts including genetic disease, excessive bodily discharges, fragility, pain, distress, dislocation of limbs, diseases related to the heart, eyes and limbs and many other general ailments. Also, Atharva Veda depicts the therapeutic and emancipative strength of water. Atharva Veda talks about water-related spirits and their influence on human life.

The Way of Life

Water as the principal element of creation is traceable in the early Vedic literature. The later Vedic texts and allied literature gave unconditional priority to water either as the sole creator, or the primary substance out of which the creator created everything else.

In the Vedic period, *Yagna* was one of the forms of worship. It was the oldest form of ritual in Hinduism before idol worship took place. *Yagna* often called fire sacrifice, is a ritual performed by a priest for invoking God and receiving certain blessings. The person who initiates the *yagna*, the *yajaman*, is the beneficiary of such receiving. During *yagna*, fire is used as a messenger to heaven, and water is used as a purifier. The water is used for making food for *yagna* and also has a prominent role in the rituals where food is treated as God and water as a goddess.

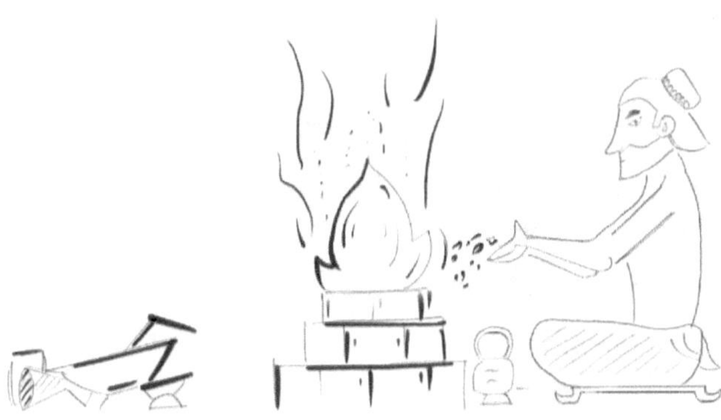

Fig-21 Yagna with fire and water

When Hinduism took the path of having more elaborate rituals, the presence of God transformed from imagination to the form of a deity. In later stages, the *yagnas* which visualized the presence of God in the ambience, changed to *poojas* and idol worship where God's presence is felt in the deity. The significance of the water also increased accordingly.

When *pooja*, a form of worship, was adopted as a daily or occasional ritual, they gave major importance to water. Often *poojas* are conducted in front of a water mug, chants are recited using water, and purification takes place in the water. Most ancient temples are constructed either on the shore of a river, lake, pond or waterfront. Devotees are asked to take dips in the water bodies for purification before entering the temples. Water from temples is treated with divinity and respect. The water used for worshipping is collected and given to the devotees for consumption as *theertham*.

There are a lot of instructions in the later Vedic literature on how to cleanse one's body with water. Many types of baths such as *naimittika*, a particular type of bath on certain occasions, *samavartana*, the bath which a student takes at the end of his studenthood, *avabhotha*, a ritual washing or ablutionary, *kamya*, a bath when the prayer is desirous of rewards, *Shraadha*, a bath taken before performing the rituals for honouring the departed etc. have been prescribed.

Nityasnana (daily bath) is recommended as a part of life and some specific ways of conducting the rituals during the baths are prescribed. It is prescribed that prayer on or with water may implore divine power. Praying during the bathing and putting on a clean unsoiled cloth later is a form of cleansing the mind, body, and erasing the sins committed by one. It is believed that water has the capacity to remove mental dirt including moral guilt, sins, or curse.

The *Grahya Sutra* literature is certain manuals detailing the religious ceremonies to be conducted at home by one who believes in Hinduism. These rituals are performed to maintain harmony, invoke blessings, and express gratitude towards the divine forces. Water plays a crucial role in many of these rituals, symbolizing purity, cleansing, and the essence of life.

Before starting any ritual, a person is required to perform *Achamana.* It involves sipping water three times while reciting specific mantras. This act symbolizes the cleansing of impurities from the body and the preparation of the mind for spiritual activities. *Pavamana* or sprinkling water is done to purify the surroundings, individuals, and objects before important ceremonies or events. *Pavamana* is done using Darbha grass or specific leaves while chanting mantras.

Tirtha prakshalana is a cleansing process with holy water that involves the ceremonial cleansing of the mouth, face and hands. It is often performed before engaging in daily prayers, or before entering a sacred space like a temple representing the symbolic meaning of cleansing oneself physically and spiritually before approaching the divine.

Pinda pradhana is another ritual where water is offered to one's ancestors by pouring water into a vessel or *Pinda,* a type of rice ball. This is accompanied by the recitation of prayers and mantras, expressing gratitude, and seeking blessings for the well-being of the ancestors. Hindus believe that this ritual helps in maintaining a connection with departed souls and ensures their peaceful existence.

Apa Upasana or meditation on water is a way of recognising water's purifying and life-sustaining qualities. *Apa Upasana* helps cultivate a deep sense of reverence for water and acknowledges its sacred role in cosmology.

Water Temples

Water holds immense significance in Hindu temples, playing a crucial role in the religious and spiritual practices of Hinduism. Apart from the sacred rivers and holy ponds, *Brahma Sarovar* is a sacred water pool situated at Kurukshetra, a city in the Haryana state of India considered a holy water pool. Taking a dip in this holy water, especially during the solar eclipse is considered to be a ritual for the ablution of sin.

Similarly, Papanasam situated on the banks of Tamara Bharani River in Tamil Nadu is revered for washing away sins. The sacred ponds in Rameswaram are sanctified water ponds for performing the last rites of loved ones and absolving earthly debts. Many other sacred water sources can be found in various locations including Banganga in Maharashtra, Bindusagar in Orissa, Pushkarnis in Karnataka, and Surya Kund in Gujarat are a few good examples of Hindu spirituality, rituals, and beliefs.

Water is considered one of the *Pancha Bhuta*, the five fundamental elements that constitute the body. Across southern India, five distinct temples have been erected, each meticulously crafted to represent one of these elements. The *Jumbukeswar* Temple, nestled in the city of Trichy, Tamil Nadu, stands as a unique sanctuary dedicated to the veneration of water in the sublime form of the *Appu Lingam.*

These *Pancha Bhuta* temples serve as sanctuaries of profound spiritual practice known as *sadhana. Sadhana* entails disciplined and dedicated efforts aimed at mastering the self and attaining higher states of consciousness. By immersing oneself in the ambience of these temples, individuals join in a transformative journey where the great five elements, integral to the human constitution, undergo a process of cleansing and purification.

Water is deeply ingrained in Hindu beliefs and highly revered for its unmatched power and diverse existence. From the primary substance of the creation to the karmic reflection of the afterlife, water is intricately woven into every aspect of Hindu life.

Chapter 11

Water – Ultimate Purifier

*"And the earth was without form and, void;
and darkness was upon the face of the deep and the
spirit of God moved upon the face of the waters."*

– The Book of Genesis, 1:2

In the ancient days of AD 28-29, the Jordan River whispered secrets as John the Baptist stood on its banks, preaching about the transformative Baptism of repentance. He saw a man with simple clothing appear from the east and approached him. John recognized the person immediately. It was Jesus.

Jesus asked John to baptize him too. But he was reluctant. Baptism was for the cleansing of sins. But Jesus, being the Son of God, was believed to be sinless. Also, Jesus was the very person John had been urging the masses to follow and he felt that baptism was not necessary for him.

John didn't want to baptize Jesus, instead, he wanted Jesus to baptize him. However, Jesus insisted and said he wanted to be baptized because he wished to submit to the commandments of his heavenly father, setting an example for those who would come after. Reluctantly, John agreed.

John guided Jesus to the Jordan River. The water embraced them, and John, with solemn purpose, took Jesus by the hand. As the waters closed over them, he intoned, *"I hereby baptise him with the authority of Almighty and you are entered into the covenant to serve him"*.

As John raised Jesus from the water, a divine spectacle unfolded. The heavens seemed to crack open. The spirit of God descended upon Jesus like a dove, declaring, *"This is my beloved Son, in whom I am well pleased. Hear ye him."*

John and Jesus stood on the banks of the Jordan River, bound by the sacred waters that had witnessed a profound moment of faith.

In the kingdom of Egypt, Hebrew tribes were entrapped in slavery under the Pharaoh. Pharaohs were threatened as they feared that one day they would be overthrown from their kingdom by a Hebrew. In a desperate bid to quell this rebellion, a sinister decree was issued—every male child born to a Hebrew family was to be ruthlessly killed.

Amidst this dark time, a Hebrew woman gave birth to a child. His name was Moses. To save him, she concealed him in a basket and set him afloat on the river Nile. The Pharaoh's daughter found him, and she took him with her. Moses was adopted into the Pharaoh's palace.

As Moses matured, a burning discontent aggravated at his soul witnessing the suffering of Hebrew members. Unable to bear the atrocities committed against them, Moses's life took a fateful turn. In a moment of fury, he killed an Egyptian slave master who had beaten a Hebrew to death. Fearing revenge, Moses fled across the Red Sea to the land of Midian. There, he encountered the divine in a most unexpected manner. The voice of God commanded Moses to go back and save the Hebrews from slavery. He obliged and returned to Egypt.

In the court of the Pharaoh, Moses pleaded for the release of the Hebrews. But the Pharaoh resisted. Then, a series of supernatural calamities occurred in Egypt. The waters turned to blood. The Egyptians suffered and started dying due to plague, thirst and hunger. Moses declared that God had unleashed these disasters as a plea for the liberation of the Hebrews.

Finally, the Pharaoh gave up and permitted the Hebrews to leave Egypt. But, as they started on their journey, the Pharaoh changed his mind, and he dispatched his army to follow and destroy them. Hebrews faced a life-threatening situation as they were trapped between the Red Sea and the approaching Egyptian forces.

In this dire moment, Moses pleaded with God for intervention and help. God asked Moses to lift his staff. He obeyed. Miraculously, the Red Sea parted, creating a passage for the Hebrews. Once they safely reached the opposite shore, Moses raised his staff again, and the sea closed upon the Egyptian army.

The Hebrews embarked on a journey towards the land of Canaan. God provided food, sending birds, and animals to feed them. However, water remained elusive. Following divine instruction, Moses struck a rock. Suddenly, water gushed from the rocks, and they managed to survive. Once they reached Mount Sinai, God revealed the Ten Commandments to Moses.

In Christianity, there is positive and negative significance of water. It is used for both giving and taking life. It remains a mysterious force and God can use his power over it. In the first Genesis, in the creation, God commanded the water to bring forth living creatures. As per Christianity water is the life-giving medium from the very beginning.

Baptism

Christian churches have an initiation ritual involving the use of water called Baptism. Baptism has two symbolic meanings. First, it is a symbol of the Hebrews being led by Moses out of slavery in Egypt. Second, it symbolises the baptism of Jesus by John.

"After Jesus' resurrection, he commanded his disciples to baptize in the name of the Father, Son, and Holy Spirit" (Matthew 28:19-20).

Baptism is regarded differently in different sects but whatever it may be baptism without water is unthinkable in Christianity.

As per Christianity, Baptism is a sign of liberation from the domination of sin that separates Christians from God. However, the Catholic Church believes baptism is not just a sign or symbolism, but a real change that occurs in humans. As per Catholicism, everyone is born sinful. The original sin is related to Adam.

As per the book of Genesis, Adam was the first man and Eve was the first woman created by God. They were allowed to eat anything other than the forbidden apple from the Tree of Knowledge. But Satan appeared as a snake. As advised by him, Eve picked the forbidden fruit and ate it. Later, she shared it with Adam too. They were expelled from paradise and sent to Earth as a curse.

The first man disobeyed God and ate the forbidden fruit of knowledge and as a consequence of the same, his sin is transmitted to all humans. They believe the stain of these original sins will be removed only when they are baptized.

The use of water in baptism is important for its value in three ways: First, it cleanses the body of any dirt or stains like how God would erase the original sin without a trace. Secondly, it fills everything it enters as God fills those who are immersed in him. Thirdly, water is required for physical survival and God is required to survive spiritually.

In the early period, baptism was normally performed with water being poured over the body while the person stood in the water. Also, most of the time the whole body is dipped into the water. This was called 'immersion', and generally, baptism is done in a flowing river or a water body. However, the acceptability of Christianity in other parts of the world paves the way for slight changes in the process. In most churches today, the baptism ceremony is performed by pouring or sprinkling water over the head.

Fig-22 Baptism

Living Water

For the Church, water is living, a concept that has a range of repercussions. The spirituality of the water in Christianity is largely based on the New Testament passages. Jesus uses the phrase "living water" on many occasions in the Bible. The first instance is found in John chapter 4.

During a journey with his disciples, Jesus sat near a well where a woman came to draw water. Jesus asked her to give them some water to drink, but the woman hesitated. Jesus was a Jew, and she was a Samaritan. The former hated the latter.

When he came to know about this, Jesus told her,

"If you knew the gift of God, and who it is that is saying to you, "Give me a drink", you Everyone who drinks of this water will be thirsty again, but those who drink of the water that I give them will never be thirsty. The water that I give will become in them a spring of water gushing up to eternal life."

Another instance is when Jesus went to the Temple to preach. He was surrounded by his disciples and worshippers. During his preaching, he suddenly called out to the crowd and said, *"If anyone is thirsty, let him come to me and drink. He who believes in me, from his innermost being, will flow rivers of living water."*

Once, Jesus met the ruler of the Jews, Nicodemus. Nicodemus asked Jesus.

"How can a man be born when he is old?"

Jesus replied.

"Surely, he cannot enter a second time into his mother's womb to be born. I tell you the truth; no one can enter the kingdom of God unless he is born of water and the spirit." *(John 3: 1-5).*

Jesus mastered water and revealed that he had a God-given authority to control and transform the universal forces. His miracles like walking on the water, calming the storms of the sea and turning water into wine were occasions that showed that miraculous things could happen with water. Many testaments said that Jesus is the "living water". He intended the phrase to mean the Holy Spirit who lived in believers and led them to salvation.

The concept and discussions of water also appear prominently concerning Jesus. He laid the command to be born again out of the water and spirit, through prayer and invocation. Jesus is also identified as a creator and life-giver. He dispenses the gift of living water.

"When Jesus was baptized, He went up immediately from the water." (Matthew 3:16 RSV) "Jesus answered, "Truly, truly, I say to you, unless one is born of water and the Spirit, he cannot enter The Kingdom of God"

Water Significance in Creation

Christianity is a monotheistic religion that follows the Psalms, Genesis, and the Bible. It might seem strange that Vedas and the Bible have some similarities even though both are from different cultures and continents. The highest similarity is the creation of the universe. In both, nothingness existed, and everything was created from this nothingness. The duality of non-existence and existence was not there at all. From nothingness, God created everything.

As per the book of Genesis, in the process of creation, God created water for Earth. He created water that rains, stores, and dries. The seven days of creation are loosely summed up in the Bible like this.

"From the beginning, even in the first act of creation, water continues to be setting the very medium of creation. After creating day and night, God turns again to the waters. He then gathers water into one place so dry land can emerge. God calls the dry land earth, calls the waters seas and then creates heavenly bodies and vegetation. This creation takes six days, and he declared on the sixth day of creation".

"Let the waters bring forth swarms of living creatures."

"God continues his creation with water as a sign of His care. He manifests a Garden in Eden, with a river flowing into it to nurture it. This river was the source of all the great rivers that graced the earth. He told water: You visit the earth and water it; you greatly enrich it; the river of God is full of water..."

Holy Water

Christianity has many aspects of water and has special spiritual effects. The blessing through water is considered for repentance, forgiveness and purification of mind, body, and soul. In the Old Testament, water was often used for ritual purifications as a symbol of spiritual cleansing and preparation.

Many churches keep holy water inside which people can sprinkle on themselves. In the biblical narrative of Exodus, the act of providing water to priests to cleanse their hands and feet upon entering the Tabernacle is an act of ritualistic importance. The holy nature of water is further emphasised in the book of Leviticus, where Aron, the high priest is advised to immerse himself in water before presenting sacrifices. In the book of Ezekiel, ceremonial washing with water symbolises attaining greater purity. In Christianity, the holy water becomes a metaphorical journey towards purification.

In earlier stages, water was used for conducting baptism. Eventually, the inclusiveness of water in various ceremonies increased. One such development was the custom of sprinkling water at mass gatherings. Today, water is used for giving blessings on many occasions, the blessings of homes, and even for the burial ceremony. Water is used for dedications, initiation of certain rituals and widely in the exorcism process.

In some Christian denominations, Water is mixed with wine during the celebration of the Eucharist, representing the divine and human nature of Jesus Christ. The combination of water and wine also reflects the redemption of humanity and reinforces the sacrificial nature of the Last Supper.

Some Christian traditions incorporate the symbolic act of foot washing during Maundy Thursday services in the holy week. It is believed that, on the fifth day of the holy week, Jesus washed his disciples' feet demonstrating humility, service, and love. The holy water serves as a powerful symbol in Christian worship, connecting believers to their faith.

Other Significance of Water

Water has both scientific and symbolic significance in Christianity. Water is raised to spiritual riches in many Christian references. Water appears in many scriptures representing refreshment, purity, prosperity, and idyllic conditions. Most importantly, water symbolizes life itself, and beyond that, God is the giver of life.

Indeed, water can symbolize salvation that brings new life. Whatever its form, the use of water reminds Christian believers that their daily blessings come from God. This includes matters such as overcoming difficulties, strength, and protection. Water is considered the most beautiful element rich in usefulness, and an excellent purifier from the filth of the body and mind.

This truth of the scientific and symbolic significance of water is found in various forms in the Christian scriptures and the prophetic books. Psalms and Ephesians are a collection of songs and general instructions basically for the unity of the church, and proper conduct in the church, home, and world.

Within the poetic verses of psalms and the teachings of Ephesians, water emerges as a powerful metaphor signifying the nature of divine guidance. Water symbolised God's word. The prophetic insights of Isaiah, the vastness of water in the sea is a symbol of the knowledge of God. Hosea, in his prophetic disclosure, implies that spring and rain are signs of the presence of God. In the book Amos, water takes on a distinct role as a symbol of social justice. Across various biblical texts, water assumes a multifaceted role, not merely a physical element but embodying spiritual truth.

In various scriptures, water is used as a blessing or as wrath. This duality reflects the positive and negative perspectives. Water, in these perspectives, becomes a tangible expression of God's grace, and the absence of water indicates divine displeasure. Whatever may be the form of the water presented, it is obvious that it is God-given and He has absolute control. Water brings Godly benefits of life in its highest order symbolising the divine presence of Almighty himself.

In Christianity, human nature is understood as a dual entity, consisting of soul and body. According to Christian teaching, Jesus instituted a two-fold purification through water and the spirit. Water with the grace of the spirit, cleanses the body from sin-making, leading them into the original blessedness. Many times, rivers and streams are associated with death and re-birth as a part of Baptism.

In the Bible, water appears more than 700 times. In the holy book, water is associated with things such as liveliness, prosperity, abundance, refreshment, and good life in general.

The Bible begins and ends with God and water. The Bible and water sustain both our physical and spiritual lives. They remind the believers about the creator and their saviour. As per Christianity, when we take water for granted, waste it, or spoil it, we suffer spiritually as well as physically. One baptismal prayer demonstrates the imagery concept of water.

"God of life through the breaking of waters and the coming of the Spirit, you bring us new birth; you give the living water, which becomes in us an eternal spring quenching our thirst, flowing through us and refreshing us for eternal life. Washed and cleansed, we are called into service with Christ.

– Uniting in Worship 2 p. 78

SHARIAH – Way to The Water Hole

"And it is He who created the heavens and the earth in six days, and his Throne was upon water".

— Qur'an 11:7

In the ancient kingdom of Babylon, Ibrahim was born as a child of a sculptor named Aazer. One eventful night, Ibrahim travelled to a nearby mountain to just watch the sky and observe nature. He never thought that this journey would change the course of his life. As he stood in the mountain, an ethereal voice enveloped him. The voice commanded Ibrahim to submit to the will of Allah. Recognising the divine call, Ibrahim bowed down and embraced Islam. His life was transformed forever, and he became a Muslim preacher thereafter.

He started spreading this word of Allah to his people. However, his own family stood divided. He told his father to embrace Islam, but his father resisted. Eventually, Ibrahim left his home and continued his journey.

His journey led him through the lands of Syria and Palestine where followers began to gather around him. One among them was a woman named Sarah. Both of them got married but the joyous union was overshadowed by Sarah's inability to conceive. Sarah couldn't bear to watch Ibrahim age without having a child and she selflessly offered her servant, Hajar, as a second wife. Soon, Hajar and Ibrahim were blessed with a son named Ismail.

But the divine plan for them was different. Following Allah's instruction, Ibrahim led Hajar and Ismail on a journey to the desolate Arabian desert. Ibrahim made Hajar and Ismail climb the Al-Marwa hill. After the climb, he made his wife and son rest under the shade of a tree and left on his journey to preach Islam. In the Arabian desert, dunes stretched for miles and there was no trace of any human habitation. Hajar and Ismail were left all alone by themselves with a bag of dates and water.

Alone in the harsh desert, days turn into a struggle for survival. Ismail, an infant, was unable to bear the inhospitable climate of the desert and was suffering. Seeing this, Hajar, desperate for help, ran between the hills of As-Safa and Al-Marwa. She ran seven times to both hills. Finally, she collapsed due to exhaustion.

Suddenly, an angel called Jibreel appeared. A miraculous strike with his foot made water gush out from the barren ground quenching the thirst of the mother and her child. This blessed spring is known as *Zamzam*.

Hajar started trading water with other travellers and survived with Ismail. Slowly, after knowing about the water resource, more settlers were attracted to this place. Makkah, the holiest city for Muslims emerged as a thriving centre. Later Ibrahim and Ismail jointly developed Kaaba, the sacred house for worshipping Allah.

Mohammedans believe *Zamzam* to be the purest water in the world. They consider *Zamzam* to be blessed by Allah and can cure all illnesses. It is also widely believed that if a person makes a wish and drinks *Zamzam* water, their wish will be fulfilled.

Fig-23 Zamzam & Kabba

Mohammed was born into a powerful tribal merchant family in Mecca, now situated in the Kingdom of Saudi Arabia. Muhammad lost his parents at an early age and was orphaned. He was raised by his paternal uncle Abu Talib and grew up with his family. Mohammed honed his skills as a merchant over the years.

Fate took a turn when he captured the attention of Khadija, a rich widow, who entrusted him with the responsibility of safeguarding her caravans to Syria. Later, a profound connection blossomed between them and eventually, they got married.

As Mohammed entered the phase of middle age, a spiritual transformation unfolded within him. Muhammad began having visions and heard voices. Seeking solitude in Mount Hira, near Mecca, he engaged in deep meditation and prayer. One day, an angel named Jibril appeared and delivered divine revelations from Allah to Muhammad.

Mohammad started sharing these revelations with the people and commenced his mission to impact these divine messages to humanity. He began laying the foundation for a burgeoning community dedicated to the newfound faith in Islam. Over two decades, Muhammad continued to receive divine guidance nurturing the growth of Islam into a prevailing force in the Arabian Peninsula. Recognised as Prophet Muhammad, he breathed his last in AD 632 leaving behind a legacy that shaped the cultural and spiritual landscapes of the region.

Shariah – The Law of Water

The Quran, revered as a sacred text of Islam, encapsulates the teachings conveyed to the Prophet directly from Allah. These revelations not only serve as spiritual guidance but also lay the foundation of Sunnah and Hadith, shaping the practice of the Islamic community. It marks the beginning and the origin of Sharia law.

Islam, which means "surrender" or "submission," was founded on the teachings of the Prophet Muhammad as an expression of surrender to the will of Allah, the creator and sustainer of the universe.

On a broad spectrum, Islam is not just a religion. It is a complete way of life and a common basis of law and personal behaviour. Sharia began to take shape and grew into a vast corpus of law. Shariah rules became a part of the law of the land and were applied by the early Muslim community. At the same time, the Shariah was also understood as a system of moral guidance for the individual believer.

Sharia is derived from the Arabic word *Shari'a*. Sharia means 'the law of water'. Its roots can be traced back to the early Arab dictionaries and originally meant "the place from which one descends to water".

In pre–Islamic Arabia, Sharia primarily comprised regulations about the use of water. The *shir `at al-maa'* were the permits that gave the right to drink water. Over a period of time, the concept of Sharia underwent evolution expanding beyond water-related guidelines to a comprehensive body of laws and rules believed to be given by God. In Islamic doctrine, water is bestowed with sacred attributes, and regarded as a source of life, sustenance, and purification. This transformation reflects a broader understanding of divine guidance and moral principles within the Islamic framework.

Muslims believe that water is the symbol of life and a divine creation flowing from paradise bestowed upon humanity by Allah for sustenance and use. In the narrative of creation, Allah created humans and all other creatures from the water. Water was the only thing in the universe before Allah created the Earth. This spiritual truth is captured in the following Quranic verse.

"We made from water every living thing."

(Qur'an 21:30).

Water Rituals

Water has a significant importance in Islamic rituals and plays a central role in various aspects of the faith. In Islam, the act of providing water to others is regarded as *Sadaqah* - a noble and voluntary form of charity.

Before starting any rituals of worship, Muslims mandatorily perform *wudu*, ritual purification with water. Purification through ablution is a fundamental component of the Islamic prayer. As a part of *wudu*, they wash their feet, arms, face, mouth, nose, and ears and smoothen over the hair and neck. This ritual signifies the importance of cleanliness and the preparation of the worshipper's body and soul before prayer.

Prayers carried out without *wudu* are considered impure and invalid.

In certain circumstances, Muslims are required to perform *Ghusl*, a full-body ritual purification using water. Muslims are required to do *Ghusl* during burial, childbirth, after sexual activities, menstruation time and so on. *Ghusl* ensures a state of purity allowing individuals to participate in acts of worship and other religious activities.

Wudu or *Ghusl* is part of *taharah, a* system of ritual purity, and it is obligatory and considered equivalent to the cleansing of body mind and soul. Some narrations indicate that anger is from *shaitan* or demons. *Shaitan* (demon) has been created from the fire and the way to extinguish the fire is to use water in the manner of making *Wudu* or *Ghusl*. Just as physical impurities are washed away, Muslims believe that acts of worship accompanied by water rituals lead to spiritual renewal. The repetitive nature of *Wudu* and *Ghusl* also serves as a reminder of the importance of constant spiritual purification and a way of life.

After using the toilet, Muslims are required to perform *istinja,* cleaning of private parts with water. Pilgrims performing *Hajj* or *Umrah*, the annual pilgrimage to Mecca, engage in various activities that involve water. From the purification rituals in Mina to the symbolic act of cleansing at the well of *Zamzam*, water is an integral part of this pilgrimage. Pilgrims often drink from the *Zamzam* well and bring back its water with them as an act of purification and blessing.

As per *Sunnah*, Muslims are advised to begin drinking water by reciting, *"Bismillah hir-Rahman nir- Rahim"* (In the name of Allah, the most gracious, the most merciful). By this act, Muslims praise Allah for giving them water to drink. After drinking, the believers are encouraged to express gratitude by reciting *"Alhamdulillah"* (All praise is due to Allah).

They are also encouraged to use their right hand while drinking. This is rooted in the belief that the left hand is associated with impurity, as it is believed that *Shaitan* does the activities with the left hand. Additionally, Muslim teachings discourage the idea of consuming water in a single gulp.

Moreover, Islamic traditions discourage the practice of drinking water while standing. This approach is considered more respectful aligning with the modesty and humility advocated by Prophet Mohammed.

Holistic Nature of Water

Islam considers water as a gift that belongs to everyone equally including humans, animals, plants etc. This inclusive concept called *Safa* envisages the shared ownership of water resources. The ethical duty of managing and protecting water resources is not merely an individual responsibility but it is woven in the fabric of communal wellbeing.

Adjacent to many mosques, a designated washing area is provided for performing *Wudu*. Certain mosques have a courtyard with a pool of clear water in the centre to facilitate the sacred ritual. In some mosques, ablution areas are found beyond their architectural confines. Fountains symbolizing purity are also sometimes found in mosques. Muslims believe God manifests through the body and looking after one's body is a way of prayer, communion, and expression of commitment to God. Water cleans the body and prayer cleanses the spirit.

The Quran and the *Hadiths* offer profound insights into the significance of water within the Islamic framework. It contains a remarkable number of specific statements about water. In the Arabic language, the term water *"ma"* recurs over 60 times in the Quran underscoring the specific religious significance in Islamic teachings.

Islam, often characterised as a comprehensive value system, extends its influence beyond ritualistic practices to embrace every aspect of life. Along with grass and fire, water is one of the three things that every human is entitled to use. Water should be freely available to all and hoarding or withholding of surplus water is an act of sin against God and humanity. The scripture highlights the moral obligation that no one should deny water to a person in need, an act will be disregarded by Allah on the day of Resurrection.

Prophet Muhammad further emphasised responsible water management. His teachings restrict the depth of water that can be utilised for irrigation. He decreed that not more than an ankle depth of water could be taken for irrigation. One ankle depth of water was considered to be sufficient for one season. Moreover, according to the *hadith,* Prophet Muhammad explicitly prohibited the act of urinating into stagnant water.

Muslim scholars have expanded on these teachings, prescribing the penalties for the misuse and pollution of water. There are two clear principles regulating water demand management in the Quran. The first is that the supply of water is fixed emphasising the need for careful supervision, and second, the water should not be wasted. These principles echo through Islamic laws, or *Shariah*, underscoring the respect that Islam instils for water a divine entity, as equal to God.

Chapter 13

Water TAO

"As a rule, whatever is fluid, soft, and yielding will overcome whatever is rigid and hard. This is another paradox: what is soft is strong."

— Lao Tzu

For a long time, ancient China was ruled and divided between many dynasties. This tapestry of dynasties wove the fabric of China, each contributing to the cultural and religious landscapes for many centuries. The ancient Chinese were deeply familiar with the forces of nature and worshipped an array of deities associated with elements such as rain, clouds, rivers, mountains, sun, moon, and earth. Among these deities, *Shang Di* held prominent positions persisting as a pivotal figure in the Chinese pantheon.

The Shang dynasty ruled China from 1600 BC to 1046 BC marking a significant era in Chinese history. Subsequently, the Zhou dynasty ascended to power from 1122 BC to 256 BC. This transformative era witnessed a major shift in the Chinese belief system. Two of the most significant changes that took place during the end of the Zhou dynasty were the birth of Confucianism and Taoism. These two belief systems had an immense influence on the advancement of basic and long-lasting principles of Chinese culture.

Lao Tzu was the caretaker of records in the Chinese royal court. He became unhappy with the prevailing state of governance and social conduct. Observing widespread corruption and ethical lapses, Lao Tzu decided to reform mankind and embarked on a mission to reform humanity. He travelled across China and Tibet and propagated a novel belief system. Lao Tzu is believed to be the founder of Taoism - a religion with its route tracing back to around 500 BC that is now embraced by over 50 million followers today. His teachings known as *"Tao Te Ching"* is a small book with 5000 characters with 81 chapters and is the manifesto of Taoism.

Taoism is a profound religious and philosophical tradition rooted in the harmonious alignment with nature. Nature worship and divination form the foundation of Taoist principles. Taoism respects the elements of wind and water. Water which embodies the softness and fluidity possessing a formidable, life-sustaining power is the symbol of Taoism. Tao means *the way* and Taoism means *"watercourse way"*.

At its core, Taoist beliefs orbit around the concept of an organizing principle governing the Universe. One can come to know the universe and cosmos by living in a harmonious existence with nature. The philosophy of Tao summarizes the fundamental nature of our existence.

According to Taoism, the spiritual discord we encounter is the result of disconnection between body, heart, and soul. The solution lies in the wisdom of Taoism, offering a pathway to reconnection and integration.

The concept of Tao means the relationship between *Yin* and *Yang,* representing the masculine and feminine energy forces, respectively. These are the forces of creation with masculine and feminine polarities.

Fig-24 Yin & Yang

As per Taoism, every face of the cosmos manifests through the dynamic interplay of *Yin* and *Yang*. Taoism embraces the "way of water". This method, mirroring the fluidity of water, aims to liberate both tangible and intangible aspects of existence. Taoism becomes a transformative journey through the "watercourse way" to seek oneness with nature.

In Taoism, a story unfolds along the bank of a mighty river, revealing the elaborate dance between man and water.

In a serene village with vast fields, an old man and his companions return after working in the fields. They were walking beside a large river. The river was flowing vigorously and wildly. Engrossed in conversation, the old man lost awareness of his surroundings and accidentally plunged into the river. The fierce current swiftly seized him. Helpless, his friends could only watch as the river carried him away.

Time passed, and just when despair gripped the friends, the old man reemerged from the water. His friends, astonished and relieved, questioned him eagerly about his miraculous survival.

"I fought against the water at first", he began.

His voice carried the weight of newfound understanding, "But then I realized it is impossible to fight and allowed myself to be carried by its flow. I wasn't harmed, instead, the water carried me".

This tale from Taoism urges us to emulate the nature of water in our lives. Water does not resist, yet it conquers all. The philosophy implores us to embrace a similar fluidity, resisting nothing, and allowing life to unfold naturally.

In the world of Tao, we should be like water and not allow anything to be enforced on us. If we force ourselves, we will invite resistance. If we resist the water and try to stop, water will find a way to flow through. Water, in its pursuit, shapes the very edges that oppose it. With time and persistence, obstruction dissolves and gives in to a smooth path. Taoism reminds us to adopt a similar approach - to be fluid, adaptable, yielding, and conquer obstacles without confrontation.

Water, tasteless and harmless, becomes a metaphor for the invisible presence of Tao. Water is life-giving and endlessly flowing. Even throughout its continuous movement, it remains clear and pure. Life is like water. It is a continuous flow, and as we navigate through our lives, we are encouraged to remain pure and clear.

We cannot step into the same water twice in a flowing river. So as per Tao, life offers no chances to rectify our mistakes. As we navigate the current of existence, Tao encourages us to tread the path with righteousness, the ideal taste of Taoist existence.

The essence of Taoist living is beautifully captured in the words of Lao Tzu:

"The best of people are like water; water benefits all things and does not compete with them. It dwells in the lowly places that all disdain—wherein it comes near the Tao."

Taoism imparts the wisdom of adopting the nature of water. Taoism teaches us to be like stagnant water when no action is required - cultivating calmness. When it's time for action, copy the adaptable nature of water. Just as water flows around obstacles, finding new channels to achieve its purpose, flow around the obstacles, and find new channels till your success gets accomplished.

The analogy of water eroding the edges signifies an invitation to embrace life with an open mind. Like water eroding the edges and dissolving them, we are urged to learn to embrace all things we meet, grow, and learn without judging. Going with the flow is a representation of forgiveness and forgetting, allowing us to transform ourselves with ease and through love.

Taoism's belief in rebirth finds a parallel in the eternal cycle of water. As per Taoism, just as water rises from the sky and returns to the Earth, our existence is seen as an unending journey of birth, death, and rebirth. Taoism says," *Our existence is eternal, and the energy never dies".*

Water is a remarkable teacher of life, providing energy and drawing a parallel concept of energy itself. Even the separation of water from the earth is always compared with energy. In its various states, whether solid, liquid, or evaporative, water remains whole - much like our energy, which persists and transforms rather than being destroyed.

Our bodies make the connection with water. It flows through us shaping us physically and subtly. It embodies the force of nature's manifestation. Without water, our body will be a mare collection of dust.

As per Taoist philosophy, water does not apply to any mortality or immortality. Water does not complain about resistance, but it simply creates a path and follows it. Water does not oppose. It is always at rest in humble places. Every drop of water mirrors the vastness of the universe. It is magnificent yet simple. Water is the Tao.

"The supreme good is like water,

which nourishes all things without trying to.

It is content with the low places that people disdain.

Thus it is like the Tao.

In dwelling, live close to the ground.

In thinking, keep to the simple.

In conflict, be fair and generous.

In governing, don't try to control.

At work, do what you enjoy.

In family life, be completely present.

When you are content to be simply yourself

and don't compare or compete,

everybody will respect you."

— Tao Te Ching

Chapter 14

WATER: Earthly & Heavenly

"All water has a perfect memory and is forever trying to get back to where it was."

— Toni Morrison

Mythological Tales

Many stories in ancient mythology describe the contest between land and water. It is a common belief that water comes to the earth from somewhere. If humans do not respect the water, it will disappear or flood and take its own turn to destroy the land and civilization. It also describes water as a kind of primaeval, mysterious force that needs to be respected for the sake of the living. In many religions, water is considered a god, goddess or semi-human figure that teaches humanity.

The Yellow River in China unleashed its destructive force, threatening to plunge the civilisation into chaos and stagnation. Faced with immense disaster, Emperor *Shun* commanded *Gun* to take charge and do something to avert the catastrophe.

Gun, under imperial command, endeavoured to construct protective embankments using soil. However, despite nine years of relentless effort, the embankments failed as the water breached the dyke. *Gun*, in his failure, met a tragic end and once again calamity reached the land.

In the wake of this setback, Emperor *Shun* called upon *Yu*, who was already assisting his father, *Gun*. *Yu* took control of the situation and decided to change the disaster management strategy. He instructed people to dig a systematic channel that effectively divided the river, mitigating its uncontrollable forces. His selfless yet dedicated and magnificent effort invited divine help. The river gods provided him with maps detailing the topography and waterways. Empowered with a mighty axe and supernatural abilities, *Yu* carved channels through mountains. He travelled around the water bodies on a 1000-year-old turtle provided to him by the gods.

After 13 years of tireless labour involving a lot of people, *Yu* succeeded in taming the flood. The digging of channels allowed water to flow in a controlled manner, and it allowed civilization to settle on the riverbanks for the next thousand years without any floods.

Emperor *Shun* recognised him as the *"Great Yu"* and appointed him as his successor in gratitude for the significant services rendered to the society. *Yu*'s rule extended for many years making the establishment of the *Xia* dynasty. Modern interpretations compare this mythical story with the flooding of the Yellow River, the deadliest flood in China which killed more than one million.

The above story bears striking similarities to the story of the king Bhagiratha as told in Hindu mythology. In this mythological tale, Emperor Sagara was blessed with 60,000 sons through the sage Aruva's boon. However, Sagara witnessed the unruliness of his sons as they matured.

Later, seeking to assert his authority, Sagara embarked on a sacred *Ashvamedha Yagna*. This grand ritual involved releasing a majestic horse after the *Yagna*, marking the territories under the kingdom's sway. The land taken by the horse will come under Sagara's rule and any attempt to impede the horse's journey was perceived as a direct challenge. A war will then decide the fate of that kingdom.

The 60,000 sons followed the horse released by their emperor father. As the sons pursued the horse, Lord Indra, aiming to teach them a lesson, stole the horse, and hid it near sage Kapila's meditation site. Mistaking that the sage had stolen the horse, Sagara's sons disrespectfully accused him, provoking Kapila's wrath. In a fit of anger, the seer incinerates all 60,000 sons with fire emanating from his eyes. Unable to perform the last rites, their spirits wander as restless souls.

Seeking forgiveness, Sagara approaches Kapila. The sage promises their liberation through *Moksha* on the condition that someone must bring the river Ganga to Earth. Ganga was flowing in heaven where the river was considered a goddess. Unfortunately, the emperor did not have any children left to do this task.

Bhagiratha was the descendant of King Sagara. He learned about his forefathers' plight and resolved to undertake this Herculean task.

After years of meditation and *Tapasya* (penance), Ganga was pleased and agreed to come down to earth. Aware of the river's immense strength which can destroy Earth, he seeks the assistance of Lord Shiva, who eventually agrees. Shiva holds Ganga in his thick hair lock and tells her that he will release her only if she respects the earth.

With Lord Shiva's intervention, Ganga flowed gently across the land, reaching the sea. Bhagiratha fulfilled his mission by immersing his forefathers' ashes in the sacred river, granting them *Moksha*, from the cycle of birth and death. This heroic endeavour has since been commemorated as *"Bhagiratha prayatna"*.

This term is used in many Indian languages to resemble the accomplishments of an impossible task. Moreover, the practice of immersing the ashes in the river, particularly the Ganga, has become a traditional Hindu funeral ritual, symbolising the belief in attaining Moksha for the departed souls.

Since ancient times, people believed that every claustrophobic disaster such as flood, drought, storm, or quake was the displeasure of Gods. These events were seen as expressions of displeasure or wrath from Gods to teach humans lessons for their sins or to purify the Earth.

One well-known example is the biblical flood, a narrative of God's action in restoring the goodness of his creation. He sends water to the Earth for 40 days and nights, flooding and wiping out entire living creatures made by him. He chose Noah, the only person God considered a good man, and told him to make a boat with his family and a pair of animals to survive the deluge. Noah's Ark, the narrative of flood, survival and subsequent human civilisation's prosperity is a widely shared mythological tale in the Abrahamic religions.

In Hinduism, a similar tale is found in the form of Lord Vishnu taking on a fish *avatar* and informing sage Manu about impending destructive floods. Following his advice, Manu built a huge ark to save the living beings. In Hinduism, Manu is regarded as the first human being. Similar flood narratives can be found in various cultures such as in China, Peru, North America, and African traditions.

Spiritual Water

The concept known as 'Living Water' is prominent in both Western and Eastern civilisations. Jainism, an ancient philosophical and religious tradition, considers that the universe consists of animate (jiva) and inanimate (ajiva), things.

Water along with plants, fire, and air are regarded as a form of non-mobile living things. Jainism is the first culture to confirm that water is produced from gases present in the air - a scientific discovery we got to know only in the 18th century. This remarkable understanding is documented in

Jain scriptures known as *agamas* with versatile details of why water is considered living and how it is produced with gases and its various forms. As per Jainism, water flowing through a river or stream is considered living, but when it is boiled, it is transformed into a non-living state. People who practice Jainism mostly consume boiling water due to this understanding.

Water is seen as a life-giving force in Buddhism and is considered a part of the four primary elements of the body. A Buddhist stupa is a shrine or a sacred monument representing Buddha's enlightenment. The stupa also can be considered as a ceremonial burial mount or a monument housing sacred relics. Stupa embodies a complex iconography with a dome and tower. These shapes incorporate geometrical pattern that symbolises five elements - fire, air, earth, water and space. The square base represents Earth, the hemispherical dome represents water, the conical spire represents fire, the lotus and crescent moon represent air, and the jewel-shaped drop or sun represents space.

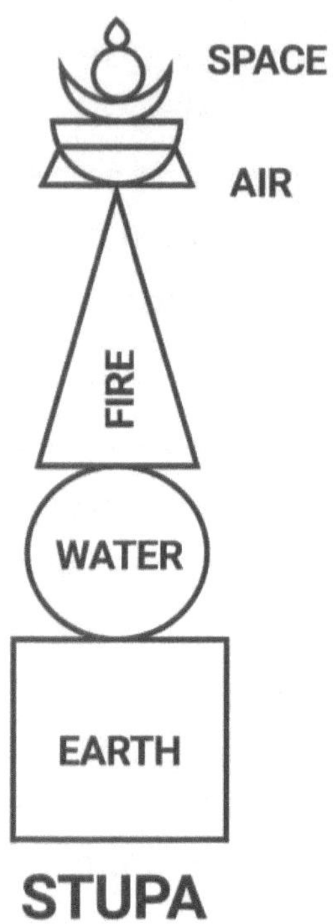

Fig-25 Buddhist Stupa

Buddhism has a tradition of bathing a little Buddha to commemorate his birth after death. Bathing Buddha is believed to help with purgation of the sins symbolising inner purification and as a medium for meditation. Bathing in water with seven items is considered to remove seven diseases and get seven blessings. In Vajrayana Buddhism, offering seven bowls of water is considered the remedy for greed as water is considered the symbol of purity.

Many times, the location of monasteries is aligned with water flow, placing sacred places upstream and social spaces downstream. Buddhism considered upstream water for spirituality and downstream water for daily use. The sound of water symbolises god's eternal life and endless magical power, and calm water is considered as a metaphor for meditation and mental purification.

Water in Buddhism is represented with sacred significance and is regarded as the main religious symbol that conveys care for all living things. The endless fountain and quiet ponds act as reference points for washing away sins, embodying ubiquity and eternity. The twin miracle with fire and water performed by Buddha is an iconic example of Buddhist belief in the existence of life and water.

Sikhism was founded in the year 1469 and is the one of most recent religions in the world. Water plays a significant part in Sikh prayer. The baptism ceremony in Sikhism is known as *"Amrut Sanskar"*. This ceremony is performed with water. The person who undergoes *Amrut Sanskar* first takes a bath, followed by drinking *'Amrut'* and having it sprinkled on their eyes. *Amrut* is prepared with water and sugar.

Gurdwaras are the spiritual place for Sikhism. Sikhism observes *miri* and *piri* addressing the spiritual and temporal aspects of life. Many gurdwaras are located near a waterfront, and taking a dip in these waterbodies is considered a practice for physical and spiritual cleanliness. Golden Temple in Amritsar, Punjab, is the holy place for Sikhism, surrounded by a pond called *Amrut Sarovar*, which means "Pool of nectar of immortality". Sikhs believe bathing in the holy waters of *Amrut Sarovar* purifies them of their bad karma.

In Sikhism, air is regarded as the teacher (Guru), water is the father, and earth is the mother of all. According to their belief, life originates from four different sources: eggs, wombs, earth and perspiration. Water is considered the origin of all these sources. God created water and air from the sun's energy and then the universe was created. According to Sikhism, life is a manifestation of the divine, with God creating life from water and infusing divine light into every heart.

Water Gods

The ancient Greeks held an unwavering belief in the celebration of heroic achievements, among which water stood as a manifestation of the divine and considered water as God. Among the 12 Olympian deities, Poseidon emerged as the formidable God of the sea. Sailors and kings prayed and offered sacrifices to Poseidon before they set sail. He is considered the husband of the earth and lord of the waters.

Many stories of Poseidon are widely told in many great manuscripts. Particularly, in the illustrious epic of Homer, namely the *Iliad* and *The Odyssey,* Poseidon occupies a centre and revered position. Poseidon's role in the *Iliad* revolves around his support for the Greeks in the Trojan War, while in *the Odyssey*, he serves as a formidable obstacle for Odysseus on his journey back home. His actions in both epics intricate the relationship between God and humans.

In ancient Aztec religion in Mexico, *Tlaloc* is the supreme god presiding over the domains of good rain, fertility, and the life-giving force of water. He was worshipped as the giver of life and sustenance. He is respected for his unparalleled domain over the elemental power of water.

The *"Tlaloc Cult"*, observed by these communities became a sacred ritual aimed at invoking a favourable rainy season and agricultural prosperity. Central to the belief of these agricultural tribes and the paramount position as the principal deity, many offerings and sacrifices are dedicated to him from those who sought his favour. The Aztecs, through their veneration of *Tlaloc*, believed that the water deity held over the prosperity of their community.

Similar to *Tlaloc*, *Chaac* is the rain God worshipped by the Mayans. They prayed to *Chaac* to send the right amount of rain. *Chaac*, with his lightning axe, strikes the cloud and produces thunder and rain. Sacrifices are often associated with *Chaac* for getting the blessing.

In Irish mythology, *Lir*, also known as *Ler*, holds the esteemed title of sea God. Another prominent God in this maritime pantheon is *Manannan*, a sea God who not only governs the island but also stands as guardian, offering protection to sailors who navigate water under his watchful gaze. Notably, *Manannan* possesses a unique power- he can grant immortality to other gods through his swine. As he gives his swine to the other gods and those who eat his swine, become immortal.

Sulis, also known as *Sul* or *Sulis Minerva*, is a water goddess revered by the Celtic tribes, the largest tribe in ancient Europe. Her presence is deeply intertwined with healing, purification, and the divine power of water. In the religious framework, the therapeutic properties of hot springs were believed to be infused with *Sulis's* divine presence.

The ancient Babylonians held a fascinating belief that the Gods emerged from the meddling of seawater with fresh water.

In Chinese mythology, *Gong Gong* is the water god who is responsible for floods and *Mazu* is the water God who protects sailors. *Ved-ava* is the water deity in Finnish mythology that is commonly associated with fishermen and generally portrayed as a mermaid.

Delving into the rich history of religious and mythological narratives around the world reveals a fascinating array of water Gods and deities. This is not limited to the culture we have discussed here. It extends to numerous other civilisations that hold water in high regard.

Across the spectrum of belief spanning from east to west and north to south, the reverence of water is profound. There are over 350 water deities dispersed throughout various ancient belief systems globally. Irrespective of these geographical or cultural differences, water consistently holds a divine status, being regarded as GOD.

Chapter 15

Water Character

"A man of wisdom delights in water."

– Confucius

The Character of Water

Ancient written languages like Sanskrit are in the form of sounds. Many modern languages are a phonetic representation of spoken words. The Chinese written language, like the hieroglyphic script of Egypt, is largely pictorial representations. This linguistic artistry conveys ideas, delineates objects, and portrays activities through a combination of basic elements that describe the intended meaning.

Chinese characters, fundamentally consist of 214 elements or radicals that incorporate elemental concepts like "metal", "hand", "head", and "person". Water in Chinese is composed of three rippled lines indicating the fluidity and dynamism of this essential element.

Fig-26 Chinese water character

This water symbol is a radical character that can combine with other radicals to produce thousands of ideas. There are more than 1600 distinct words in the Chinese language wherein the water radical appears. As per Confucian texts, water is a symbol of benevolent necessity of life. This Ideology considered water as the "source of life".

Feng Shui

The cosmological system and traditions that developed in Chinese traditions over centuries provide great insights into water. The system states that the universe is composed of dynamic energy that operates in two modes, *Yin* and *Yang*, two polarities where *Yin* represents masculinity and *Yang* represents femininity.

These modes interact to create five types of basic energies - fire, water, earth, wood, and metal. These five configurations of energy combine and recombine to produce a lot of things and form the building block of the universe. Any changes in the universe occur by addition or subtraction of *Yin* and *Yang* energy.

Most Chinese practices assume that the earth is filled with energy and there are specific sites possessing heightened energy levels. These energized places are ideal for human habitation. *Feng shui,* a widely used system, means wind and water, helps identify these energetic locations for various purposes for building cities, temples, houses and even locating graves. The typical site was characterised by an abundance of *Yang* energy of the sun (fire) and the *Yin* energy of flowing water. In such sites, it was believed to have prosperity, good fortune, and a life free of diseases and accidents.

Vastu Shastra

Vastu shastra, the science of architecture, is a traditional Indian system that encompasses a comprehensive principle governing the design, layout, measurement, ground preparation, and design theories. This traditional system of architecture is not a set of guidelines but rather constitutes a rich tapestry of ideas, theories and concepts that aim to integrate architecture with nature. Both *Vastu shastra* and *Feng shui* are based on powerful cosmic energies.

Vastu revolves around the harmonious interplay of five fundamental elements: Water, Fire, Air, Earth, and Space. While Earth and water pose constraints on habitat availability, Fire (Sun), Air, and Space are universally accessible. Considering this, *Vastu* is the science of balancing these five elements in an appropriate proportion to keep perfect harmony. Each element interconnects with others, and *Vastu Shastra* serves as the systematic study of aligning these elements to absorb positive vibrations and usher in a flow of energy conducive to harmony, peace, and good health.

The interdependence of these elements is elegantly illustrated in the elemental cycle. Water gives rise to air. Air helps fire to burn. Fire transforms into ash and begets earth. Earth solidifies into metal, also called space and space, in turn, evaporates to form water.

According to *Vastu Shastra*, each direction is associated with an element and water is associated with the north and east direction. Water is linked to prosperity and fertility. A location blessed with free water flow is considered auspicious for habitation according to *Vastu Shastra*. Also, water serves as a remedial element for rectifying the imbalance of other elements and harmonising their effects to promote a balanced and contemporary living.

The Metric System

Until the French Revolution happened, most of the world used various kinds of systems to measure and weigh. These methods were inconsistent and often led to frequent disputes among traders, merchants, and the general population as varying standards existed in different regions, causing confusion and discord.

Recognizing the need for a universal standard, the creators of the metric system wanted to choose units that were logical and practical. They decided to derive the properties of natural objects. In this pursuit, water emerged as a reference point due to its consistent physical characteristics worldwide.

The metric system creators opted for a logical foundation, designating water as the reference for size, weight, and volume units. Notably, one litre of water becomes synonymous with one kilogram. The freezing point of water is established as 0 degrees Celsius while its boiling point is designated as 100 Degrees Celsius. The density of water, set at 1000 kilogram per m3 equivalent to 1000 litres of water. With this reference, the world got an efficient and harmonised global approach to measurement. The metric system becomes the first widely accepted measurement unit.

Water Clock

Ever since humans understood the time, a device for measuring the time was essential to them. Initially, they measured the time by the movement of the sun, moon, and stars. The most popular method was observing the sun's rays. As the sun moves, shadows change the directions and lengths, and a sundial was developed to measure the time. However, the accuracy of the sundial was not proper as the length of the day varies at different seasons. Subsequently, oil lamps and candle clocks were developed. But again, their reliability was compromised by factors such as the quality of oil and wax, leading to unreliable readings.

Water clocks, also known as *clepsydra*, were invented by about 1500 B.C.E. This device relied on a steady flow of water, either into or out of a container. Time could be measured by the markings in the container. The *clepsydra* proved to be a reliable timekeeping tool and was widely used across cultures and regions. The mechanical clock was invented in the 12th century and eventually replaced the *clepsydra*.

Zodiac Signs

The concept of Zodiac signs traces its origin back to Babylonian astronomy emerging almost 3000 years ago. It subsequently transitioned into Hebrew and Greek astronomy. Today, it is widely accepted in Western astronomy and astrological practices. The zodiac signs are an astronomical coordinate system specifying the positions of planets. As per zodiac astrology, each planet represents a facet of one's personality.

There are 12 zodiac signs and one's personality is largely influenced by the house of planets you were born in. Your astrological destiny relies on planetary positions and is based on the zodiac signs of four elements - Fire, Water, Earth, and Air.

Among these, three zodiac signs represent water - Cancer, Scorpio, and Pisces. The basic characteristics of the person born with the above zodiac signs are like the character of water from an astrological point of view. They display remarkable adaptability in various situations, possess a lovable nature, boast high emotional intelligence, engage in serious relationships and so on. The inherent qualities associated with water signs align with the dynamic and transformative nature of water.

Fig-27 Water Zodiac signs

Similar to the Babylonian and Western astronomy and astrology, Indian Astrology also employs a classification of systems based on four fundamental elements. These elements impact their distinct qualities to the 12 *Rashis* or Astrological signs. Also, this elemental categorisation extends to the planets as well.

The *rashis* associated with water elements are *Karkataka*, *Vrishika* and *Meena.* Correspondingly, the planets linked to water elements are Moon, Venus, and Jupiter. The planetary arrangements of these planets with the corresponding *rashis* played a vital role in determining the proportion of each element present in an individual's horoscope and shaping the unique characteristics and traits.

Chapter 16

Water & Our Generation

------- ❧❧ -------

"The earth, the air, the land, and the water are not an inheritance from our forefathers but on loan from our children. So, we have to hand over to them at least as it was handed over to us."

– Mahatma Gandhi

In ancient Greek, Roman, and Mesopotamian narratives, the achievement is celebrated and considered near to godliness. In Abrahamic narratives, submission and discipline are considered godliness, and in Asian narratives, seeking and understanding are celebrated as the same. Depending on this belief system, the importance of water is also managed. But in conclusion, all understand the importance of water and consider it as an "elixir of life".

We have not known our water for a long time. We do not know about the journey of water through oceans, rivers atmosphere etc. Whatever, we have today is the result of a water's journey on earth. The movement of water in and around the earth decides the climate and makes earth a habitable place. The large water bodies and ocean started interacting with the atmosphere and all this for over a million years made the earth habitable for living beings.

Water and Sun helped the photosynthetic process and plants started growing on land. The water in its journey carried the nutrients and minerals which were distributed in the land for creating a fertile ground required for vegetation to grow and sustain.

The journey of water, which we call the water cycle or hydrological cycle is known as the largest movement on earth. These cycles take approximately 3100 years to complete, with ocean water evaporating into the atmosphere. Fortunately, nearly all of this water is returned to Earth through precipitation. Without this constant replenishment, the oceans would disappear in 3100 years.

One of the pressing issues today is global warming with a focus on the rising temperature of the oceans. Between 1976 to 2012, the surface temperature of the oceans increased by 0.59 °C, with the Atlantic Ocean warming even more over 1°C. An increase in surface temperature will interchange the energy between the oceans and the atmosphere. This means, that as the oceans warm, there is an increase in evaporation, leading to more precipitation. This results in bigger storms in various parts of the world. Also, the rise in sea level contributes to the melting of glaciers and ice sheets., causing flooding of coastal cities. Today, around 40% of deaths and societal costs of natural disasters are the results of floods.

The journey of water was extremely important for civilisations to survive and prosper. Many civilisations culminated, thrived, and collapsed, but the journey of water continues and shall do so for centuries to come. In the above journey, water is constantly on the move from one part to another purifying the earth and making sure that fresh water is available for growth.

But today, most people assume that water is mere H_2O, and judge its implications for our health solely upon the chemical and bacterial analysis. We consume water only for thirst. We consider water a cheap commodity. We fight over it. We might pay our water tax. Yet, we misuse water on a daily basis. We complain about heat waves in summer and later whine about floods during monsoon.

Water is a cheaply available liquid today. For humans, water is used for cleaning, drinking, and cooking. For industry, it is a cheap commodity used for processing, power generation, heating, and cooling. For the government, it is the source of power, conflict, and vote bank politics. For the world, it is a geopolitical concern and a source of conflict and power. We are possibly staring at a third world war to conquer and possess water.

Today, water exploitation and pollution emerge as a global challenge. Whatever fresh water is available to us, 70% of it is utilised for agricultural purposes. Out of this, as per a rough estimate, 30% of water is used in livestock maintenance, while 40% is used for cultivating plant-based products.

Unfortunately, 40% of the water used in agriculture is dissipated through evaporation, runoff from fields, and lost during transit. Additionally, another 20% is wasted due to antiquated irrigation practices, mismanagement, and negligence, amounting to a total wastage of 60%. By implementing water conservation measures, this substantial water can be redirected to areas where it is desperately needed. However, most of the government policies focus on farm subsidies, neglecting crucial actions related to water conservation.

Industrial water consumption accounts for approximately 17% of the total fresh water available to us today. However, a significant portion of this water, mostly more than half, is discharged as untreated effluent, posing environmental hazards. Less than half of the water used in industries undergoes some treatment, with the majority being discharged to open sources. Merely, 11% of water is recycled and reused.

Similarly, the domestic water sector consumes 12% of the freshwater, of which a major quantity is discharged without any treatment. The attention given to effective water treatment in these sectors is still insufficient on a global scale. If we take out more fresh water than nature can replace, the amount of fresh water will decrease, causing scarcity.

Our perception of water consumption is often limited to 3 to 5 litres per day. But the reality is more complex and surprising. When we account for the factor of water used in the production of our food, the water consumption will expand significantly, reaching approximately one litre per calorific value consumed. If we stick to a 2000-calorie diet, we indirectly use around 2000 litres of water. This is because water is an essential component in the production of various foods.

For example, the production of 1 kg of beef requires 15000 litres of water. Similarly, every kilogram of cheese involves 5700 litres, and the production of 1 Kilogram of rice demands approximately 2500 litres of water. Even everyday items like a sheet of paper have a water cost, using 10 litres per sheet.

Apart from this, daily, an individual's average water consumption varies from 50 to 600 litres based on water-rich and water-poor regions and the country's development index. Average daily water consumption is roughly 150 to 200 litres in India and 350 to 600 litres in the US. This consumption trend is on the rise, but unfortunately, the availability of fresh water is rapidly declining.

Our ancient belief systems have taught us something different. They taught us to respect water. Because it is not as a simple liquid as it is known to be. They understood the power. Not the power of flood or calamity, but of influence, love, and gratitude. The power which can influence our mind body and soul. An amazing power that you experience daily.

Now, I am going to tell you all the secrets of this influence and ideas for life. I will be sharing with you, how as an individual, as a family, as an organisation, and as a society, make use of this boon to improve your life in dynamic ways.

Many people have already understood this. Many are already using this to their benefit and are gaining from it. Now, it is your time to understand it! Without further ado, let's move on to the second part of our book.

Water – Ideas for life

"If we wish to die well, we must live well"

– Anonymous

Chapter 1

As You Sow So Shall You Reap

*"All actions take place on the stage of the time by
the interweaving of the force of Nature".*

– Bhagwat Gita

Our earliest ancestors prioritized securing food, shelter, and water for survival. In their pursuit, they roamed in search of water and hunted for sustenance. As they recognised the significance of fire for cooking, they developed an early concept of storage and food safety,

With a growing understanding of agriculture, our ancestors stopped wandering and started settling in one place. They built their homes near water bodies to take care of crops and personal needs. Slowly, they created small cities on the shore of water bodies and in this way, a civilisation came into being.

Various civilisations such as the Egyptians along the Nile River, the ancient Chinese along the Yellow River, the Mayans along various cenotes, the Mesopotamians along the Tigris and Euphrates Rivers and Indians along the Indus and five rivers, flourished in close proximity to water.

Sooner, these civilisations adapted their own relationship with water. Instead of spreading the civilisation near water bodies and rivers, they brought water to their settlements. Irrigation helped to build early communities and this networking was the catalyst behind the growth of civilization.

Water was one of the important learning grounds for building society. Our ancestors understood the power of gravity and they made channels, canals, and tunnels to bring water to their settlements. Hydrology was born in this way and slowly our civilisation started controlling the water flow.

Once the understanding of hydrology was clear to our ancestors, they progressed from small settlements to developing larger cities. They engineered reservoirs, dams, ponds, manmade lakes, and various water structures. Soon, controlling of water became conquering. This was done in a very harmonious way for centuries and there was an informal understanding between water and our ancestors.

As our civilisation expanded across the vast expanses, the water demand experienced a staggering surge. In response, they innovated novel methods for storing and regulating water. Together with major technological improvements and industrialisation, the usage of water diversified into many areas including industrial processes, electricity generation, organised agricultural activities and so on. We changed the hydrological way of handling water transport.

Later, our approach towards the transportation of water through canals and manmade streams underwent a transformative shift. The canals and streams were replaced with a more dynamic system driven by pressure and force. We erected huge pumping stations and transported the water through pressurised pipes.

As the urban population burgeoned, natural lakes vanished, replaced with artificial reservoirs. The flow of the river was reduced due to large dams across them. The riverbed shrunk due to land encroachments. Eventually, we forgot the fundamental aspects of water taught by our ancestors. Water soon became a simple commodity. Respect became contempt.

Water has faced severe disrespect and abuse over time. While our ancestors revered and respected water, subsequent generations have polluted and disrespected it. Billions of litters of polluted water containing industrial effluents, human waste, sewage, and various other pollutants are discharged into the water bodies daily. Unfortunately, our water bodies have become dumping grounds.

It was only during the 20th century, that we started to talk about water pollution and its scarcity seriously. By this time, many cities were experiencing some or other problems related to water. This gave an acceleration in a more vigoured way to solve these problems. Today, extensive water and wastewater treatment facilities exist, accompanied by strict discharge standards.

The transportation of water across cities, sometimes spanning thousands of kilometres has become a day-to-day affair. The transportation of water from water-rich to water-poor areas has become a routine, facilitated by multiple pumping stations.

Centuries of pollution, exploitation, and negligence affected our water flow. Many rivers no longer flow, streams and lakes have dried up, and the water table has dropped. This has led to a serious water scarcity crisis. Densely populated cities and many parts of the world are facing severe water shortages. These issues are going to worsen in future which can lead to conflicts over water resources. There's widespread worry about water pollution and water scarcity. It is a major concern everywhere.

However, the fundamental nature of the water remained constant over time. The water we have now is essentially the same as when Earth began with water.

By asserting the rate at which water molecules in the atmosphere break down into hydrogen and oxygen, we can estimate the water loss. Hydrogen, being lightweight, easily escapes into space once separated from oxygen. This effect decreases the amount of water vapour in the atmosphere. Calculations show that only about 0.2% of the water in the ocean has been lost to space since the beginning of the earth. This means that most of the water we see on the earth today was the very same as when the earth began with water.

Fortunately, the water lost to space is replaced by the same geological processes, maintaining the overall balance. The mass of water in today's ocean is equivalent to the mass present in the earth's crust when the degassing process began.

In terms of percentage, the water on earth is distributed as,

Oceans – 97.3%

Polar Ice and glaciers- 2.1%

Underground aquifers – 0.5%

Lakes and rivers – 0.01 %

Atmosphere – 0.001 %

Biosphere – 0.00004%

The percentage of water mentioned above, only 1.3% of the Earth's water is available for human consumption. A significant portion of this freshwater is inaccessible, locked up in ice lakes and rivers. However, researchers now think that more water, about 30 times the quantity of current ocean water, is hidden in the Earth's bowels. But when we can access this water, only the future can tell us.

Traditionally, rivers, wells and lakes have been a vital source of water for us. That's enough for us to survive if we do not spoil or pollute them. However, our current practices are jeopardising this essential resource. Our careless use, contamination, and wasteful habits are contributing to water scarcity, prompting concerns about even more severe draughts in the future. Nevertheless, a crucial factor, on par with pollution and scarcity, is the neglect and detachment we exhibit in relation to "Our Life with Water".

Today, much of our water resources are depleted or contaminated, forcing us to rely on chemically treated water for various purposes. This was initially limited to urban areas but now, even rural populations have no choice but to consume chemically treated water.

This water, delivered through pressurised pipelines, has become ubiquitous in our daily lives. We carry bottled water everywhere and use pressurised water for cooking, bathing, and drinking. Unfortunately, this treatment and transportation process alters the water significantly, stripping it of its natural characteristics and vitality. Water undergoes extreme changes influenced by confined spaces, elevated pressure, rapid velocity, intense turbulences, and frictional forces. The life and energy inherent in water are compromised during this process. At the end of the day, we consume *"dead water"*.

We have contaminated water in various ways and continue to use it, believing it to be pure after physical, chemical and biological treatment. However, the overlooked reality is that we are essentially using *"dead water"*.

Our concern should not be limited to water shortage or pollution. A more significant worry lies in understanding the repercussions of using contaminated and lifeless water on our physical, mental, and spiritual health. I term it *"cosmic contamination"*.

Our life begins and survives with water. Considering that all living organisms on earth are comprised of it, water's role extends beyond our birth and survival. Water possesses the power to influence our body, mind, and energy. It can shape our character, emotions, behaviour, functions, and feelings. Water is a constant companion and potential adversary, affecting us not only physically but also on a physiological, intellectual, logical, and emotional level.

The way we treat water determines its behaviour and we inevitably face the consequences when we abuse it. Understanding the principle of "As you sow, so shall you reap" applies perfectly to the state of water. By viewing water from a different perspective, one can unlock numerous possibilities for well-being. It will give you a whole lot of purpose. However, to reap the benefits, water must be used mindfully.

My whole idea of writing this book is about revealing this perspective and offering practical ideas for incorporating water into your life. That is why this book is titled, *"Water-Ideas for Life"*.

The first part delves into the water, while the second part explores the relationship between you and water.

Chapter 2

Body of Water

"Thousands have lived without love,
not one without water".

— Wystan Hugh Auden

The great *Kurukshetra* war unfolded its fateful chapter, and the air crackled with the stench of impending death. The Pandava army found itself ruthlessly crushed under the force of the Kauravas. Led by Dronacharya, Kauravas employed a diabolical strategy called *chakravyuha* - a unique formation comprising men, elephants, chariots, and horses arranged like a lotus flower. It was a formidable maze, and breaking through it required specialised skills and knowledge. Because of this *chakravyuha* formation, the Kauravas were protected, secured, and progressed towards Pandavas and literally massacred their army.

In the heart of Pandava camp, discussions were rife among the war-weary commanders and brothers. Arjuna, the renowned archer and the only one among Pandavas skilled enough to dismantle the *chakravyuha* found himself persistently engaged by the rival Kaurava forces. Drona was aware of Arjuna's expertise, and he strategically arranged his army to prevent Arjuna from breaking the formation.

On the 13th day of the intense war, tension filled the Pandava camp. Abhimanyu, Arjuna's son, entered the army tent. The 16-year-old warrior sensed the urgency of the situation and confidently said, "I know how to break the *chakravyuha*".

His bold statement was doubted. "How do you know this?" Inquired the gathered commanders. "The secret is known only to Drona. Your father was his favourite disciple and he taught Arjuna the art of breaking *chakravyuha*. No one else possesses that knowledge", they argued.

Abhimanyu, wise beyond his teen years, explained. "When my father was training with Drona, I was in my mother's womb. Excited to share something special, every day, my father would narrate the formation of *chakravyuha* to my mother Subhadra. One day, he detailed the steps of breaking it, and those words seeped into me as I floated in my mother's amniotic fluid. I remember every step".

Fig-28 Abhimanyu listening from his mother's womb

The Pandava commanders were now convinced of Abhimanyu's conviction. However, they were unaware of the fact that the brave teenager only knew how to break into the *chakravyuha* but wasn't aware of the tactic to escape once inside it. Nevertheless, the Pandava camp was desperate for a breakthrough.

On the day of war, Abhimanyu managed to pierce the *chakravyuha*. He caused chaos among the Kaurava forces and killed many prominent warriors. It was a moment of triumph for the Pandavas as the *chakravyuha* crumbled under the young warrior's onslaught.

However, furious at the unexpected turn of events, Drona and Kauravas abandoned the rule of war. They surrounded Abhimanyu and killed him mercilessly. The rules of the war were repeatedly broken in the chaos that followed

Abhimanyu's demise. By the end of the 18th day, the Pandavas emerged victorious in the *Kurukshetra* war.

This tale from the epic *Mahabharata* is a fantastic example of our deep connection with water. The relationship extends far beyond the conventional realm, delving into chemical, physical, biological, mental, spiritual, cosmical, and mythical dimensions. Whatever it may be, water is a major player in our life.

Among its numerous roles, one of the crucial roles which water plays in our lives is memory. Water holds the thread of our recollections. Perhaps, it is this extraordinary ability to retain information that allowed Abhimanyu to grasp the war strategy from his mother's womb. In part one of this book, the memory of water is extensively explained. Still, it is a very controversial subject. But, as we navigate the fluid pathway of our existence, a proper understanding of our association with water comes to light, shredding new perspectives on the significance of this vital relationship.

First, let's explore the relationship between our bodies and water to give more light on the pathways where water courses through the very fabric of our being. Let's go where the water flows through us.

When we are in our mother's womb, 99% of our tiny body is made of water. We were surrounded and protected by a bag of water called amniotic fluid. The uterus will accumulate amniotic fluid from the first trimester onwards and will have 800 to 1000 millilitres of amniotic fluid during the final stage of pregnancy.

This amniotic water shields us from harm, preventing injuries and infections. It also plays a crucial role in the development of our digestive systems, lungs, bones, tissues, and muscles. Amniotic water is not just a shield, it is the carrier of essential nutrients, hormones, and antibodies that contribute to our growth and well-being in our womb stay. This watery environment ensures our comfort by regulating temperature regardless of the external weather conditions. Throughout our time in the womb, we drank this water and breathed in it.

When the amniotic fluid breaks, it marks the beginning of our journey into this world. At birth, our body and organs are still 90% water. In essence, our life began in the water.

From the moment our life begins, our bodies undergo various water-related changes crucial for both physical and mental development with sophisticated and complex mechanics. Water regulations mainly happen in three key stages: foetal development, throughout growth and in our ongoing lives.

By adulthood, about 65-70 % of our body is water, depending on our age. All our organs consist mainly of water. Even the robust skeletal structure contains significant water content. When we examine our bodies, we can find some surprising facts about the water content. We are essentially a water container.

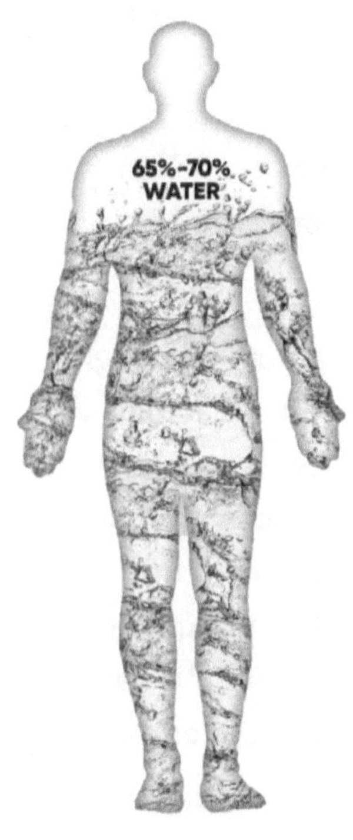

Our blood is 50% water.

Our kidney is 80-85% water.

Our liver is 70-80% water.

Our lungs are 75- 83% water.

Our muscles are 70-75% water.

Our brain is 80-85% water.

Our skin is 70-75% water.

Our tissues are 70% water.

Our bones are 20-25% water.

Our fat content is 20-25% water.

Our Heart is 75 to 80 %water.

Fig-29 Our body & water

In a day we normally drink about 2 to 3 litres of water. Another 1 or 2 litres will be absorbed by our bodies when we bathe. Some more percentage of water will enter the body through the food we eat. So, on average, we consume a significant amount of water, an average of 3 to 5 litres, or even more. This consistent water intake goes beyond mere hydration and thirst quenching. An array of activities which is very much essential for sustaining our life is done by water in our body.

Water comprises 65 to 70% of our body mass evenly distributed to take care of the balance of our body. Looking at it another way, the human body consists of 65 to 70% water and 30 to 35% solids. This water content serves as a vital facilitator for fundamental bodily functions. It facilitates life itself.

All biological activities in our body are the results of actions from the water. Water is a dynamic medium within our bodies that dissolves, reacts, dilutes, transports, and interacts with each bodily function. To comprehend the sophisticated relationships between our body, mind, and water, it is imperative to delve deeper into the exploration of these processes. Let us embark on a journey to unravel the deep connections between our bodies and the omnipresent element - water.

Chapter 3

The Flowing Water

"In time and with water, everything changes."

— Leonardo da Vinci

Water is a colourless, tasteless, and odourless substance with no calorific values. But it is often regarded as the most important nutrient. We can't survive more than 5 days without water. In our simple knowledge, water is an inorganic substance composed of two hydrogen atoms bonded with one oxygen atom. We know drinking enough water will hydrate us adequately. Let's explore, what exactly happens within our bodies when we consume water.

Shocking water

Our bodies absorb water through the intestines and distribute it all over the body in the form of body fluids. When we consume water, this water contains several electrolytes. The main electrolytes are calcium, magnesium, sodium, potassium, chloride, sulphates, and carbonates. These minerals are required for many functions of the body and hence, drinking water is also called mineral water. The presence of these minerals measured as dissolved solids imparts electric conductance to water. Consequently, when electricity passes through our bodies, we experience an electric shock. Pure water without any dissolved solids or minerals does not conduct electricity. When water is in our body, it acts as an electrical conductor.

Bloody Water

The human body contains approximately 5 to 6 litres of blood for men and 4 to 5 litres for women. This is about 7 to 8% of our body weight. Blood is a thick fluid with a viscosity ranging from 3.5 to 5.5 cP (centipoise) plays a crucial role in our physiological balance. It maintains a pH balance between 7.35 to 7.45, indicating a slightly alkaline nature. Any value below 7 is considered an acidic nature, while a value above 7 signifies alkaline nature.

Blood comprises 55% liquid and 45% solid components including several types of cells. The primary liquid component is plasma, constituting 90 to 92% of water. Effectively, our blood is a significant part of water. This plasma, a straw-coloured fluid serves as a medium in which blood cells are suspended, facilitating their transport throughout the body.

Blood serves as our body's transport system. It carries essential substances like oxygen and nutrients and removes waste products such as carbon dioxide. Blood circulates through the body three times every minute, covering an impressive distance of 19,000 km in a day. Water also travels similarly as 55% of blood and 90% of plasma is water.

Oxygen, which is very crucial for our cell function is less soluble in water. Hence, the cells require more oxygen for their proper functioning. However, red blood cells (RBC) can carry much more oxygen that can be dissolved in blood. Haemoglobin, a protein found in RBCs, has an affinity with oxygen. This happens with the assistance of iron presence in the haemoglobin. Iron gives the blood its red colour.

However, iron has a high affinity towards carbon monoxide, a low molecular gas produced by the body as a byproduct of heme metabolism. Carbon monoxide binds haemoglobin and blocks oxygen binding and transport by haemoglobin in the bloodstream. Eventually, carbon monoxide becomes carbon dioxide and further becomes carbonic acid which can disrupt the pH balance. If the blood's pH drops below 7.3, it loses the ability to carry carbon dioxide and a further reduction in pH can be fatal, causing coma or death. Blood needs to maintain this pH buffering for our survival.

Water plays a major role in this process of pH balancing. When carbon dioxide dissolves in the blood, water gives hydrogen ions forming carbonic acid. This weak acid quickly breaks down into hydrogen and bicarbonates. Bicarbonates are slightly alkaline which helps to counteract the acidity and keep the blood pH within its optimal range.

The Lubricator & Shock Absorber

You might have come across the term "Wan Der Waals force". In molecular chemistry, this force dictates how atoms and molecules interact based on their distance from each other. It is an attraction or repulsion between molecules. Water molecules will resist when they are forced together, exhibiting Wan Der Waals force.

Remarkably, this force plays a crucial role in our bodies, functioning as both a lubricant and shock absorber. This significance of Wan Der Walls force becomes evident in our joints, Here, water acts as a cushion and eliminates the friction between the joints. This cushioning effect is vital for smooth joint movement, enabling the surface to slide and glide seamlessly. For those experiencing arthritic pain, increasing water intake is often recommended by doctors to harness the lubricating power of water.

The lubrication process with water extends beyond joints. Saliva, spinal cords, body cells, and eyes, all benefit from its lubricating properties. Saliva water, for instance, provides essential lubrication to our mouths and food pipes. In our eyes, water serves as a cushion, maintaining the optimal pressure on the retina and lens. In our spinal cords, water acts as an awesome shock absorber.

Water surrounds the brain area to protect it from any shock or trauma. Moreover, water functions as a protective barrier for nerve cells, enhancing their functionality and safeguarding sensitive compounds within the cell from external chemical reactions. Water also acts as a lubricant for the respiratory and digestive tract as well as various tissues throughout the body. We have already discussed amniotic water and foetus protection in the previous chapter.

The Cooler

Our bodies are very sensitive to the temperature both internally and externally. Our ideal body temperature is 37 degrees Celsius or 98.6 degrees Fahrenheit. We can have a narrow range in the body temperature between 36.1 to 37.2 Degrees Celsius or 97 to 99 degrees Fahrenheit. We have only this narrow comfort zone for our well-being. The water within our plasma plays a crucial role in maintaining this optimal temperature.

Our body cleverly employs water as a coolant to regulate temperature. Hypothermia and Hyperthermia are the terms used for temperature abnormality. Hypothermia indicates low body temperature and hyperthermia refers to high body temperature. When the temperature is high, the body's enzymes stop functioning leading to muscle failures and the collapse of our nervous system. Depending on the body's conditions, sweat and water act as body coolants. Water is an efficient mechanism for storing heat. Water has a high specific heat index. Since our bodies are composed of 65 to 70% water, body temperature occurs slowly and gradually due to water's ability to store heat. This quality helps to regulate our body temperature.

When excess heat is generated in the body, the body routes the blood to skin capillaries and water is converted to a vapour through sweat. As the water evaporates from the skin, the body cools. Here, water acts as a thermoregulator.

The Chemist and Biologist

The biological significance of water in our body is very fundamental, as it plays a crucial role in biological and chemical processes. Water contains no calorie content. However, it is the medium for most metabolic reactions involved in energy production. Metabolic reactions are chemical reactions happening in our bodies. The food we eat will change into energy due to metabolic reactions. The usability and absorbability of protein and carbohydrates during the digestion process depend on the water-associated chemical reactions.

Water functions as a solvent for blood and serves as the backdrop for various metabolic reactions. One of the basic reactions is related to proteins and carbohydrates. Proteins, the building block of our body, attain their functional shape through sequences of amino-acid reactions with water. Proteins are synthesized as a long chain of building blocks called amino acids. These building blocks need a specific shape for their proper function. Water holds these specific shapes. Protein provides structure and catalytic reactions in the cell that leads to many major functions including communication and muscle contractions. The shape of the protein is vital to perform these functions and water provides that shape.

Water's role as a medium for chemical reactions is further heightened by its high heat-holding capacity and universal solvent nature. Our body uses water as an agent for enzymatic reactions. Proteins and DNA are made as repetitive units of small molecules. Water is required for the joining and breaking of these molecules. The joining action produces the water, and the breaking action requires water. These actions are required for the cells to obtain nutrients and repurpose big molecules.

Moreover, water acts as a buffering solution for the cells, adapting to the cell's requirements by acting as an acid or base. In response to specific cellular needs, water molecules give up the hydrogen and become OH or accept another hydrogen and become H_3O. This buffering capability protects the cells from the potentially harmful effects of acidic or basic conditions. Water neutralizes the effect and protects protein and other molecules in the cell. No other substance possesses such versatile characteristics crucial for sustaining our life.

The Cellular Friend

The fluid medium inside our cell called cytoplasm is mostly water. Water plays a pivotal role in cellular biology, influencing the function of red and white cells. Red blood cells are responsible for oxygen transport and white blood cells are essential to the immune system. Both types of cells, suspended and transported in plasma, owe their mobility and functionality to the presence of water. Water fills the cell and allows everything inside the cells to keep the right shape. In the biochemical process, it is crucial to maintain their shape at the molecular level. Moreover, water creates enough pressure inside the cells, helping to resist any external forces. It acts like a protector to save our cells from damage.

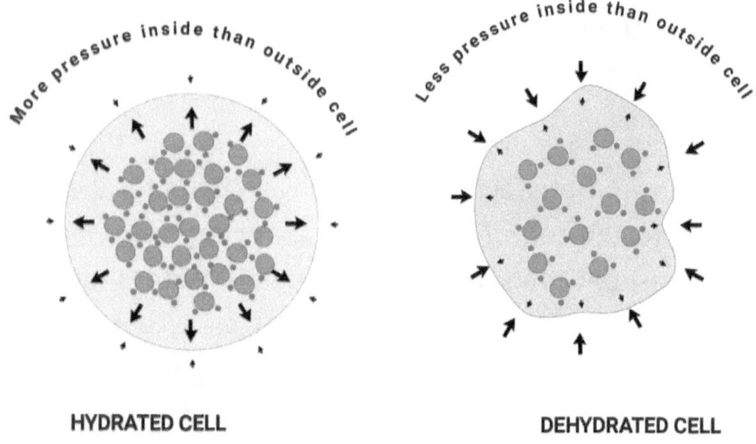

Fig-30 Hydrated and dehydrated cell

The inner part of the cells is rich in glucose. However, the size of the glucose molecules is too big to pass the cell membrane fabric, hampering their outward dispersions. Here too, water plays a crucial role driven by osmosis.

Osmosis is a phenomenon happening in our bodies all the time. It controls the movement of water from one area to other areas around the body based on the pressure, temperature, and concentration of electrolytes. Osmosis is the maintenance of equilibrium in the body. Water enters the cell and equalises the glucose concentration, leveraging the pressure differential induced by osmosis. Either side of the membrane creates an osmatic pressure prompting water to enter the cell and neutralise it.

The same process happens when we take nutrients and salts. If the body fluids outside our cells become high with salts, osmosis takes water from the cells. This creates a state of dehydration in our bodies. This explains why consuming seawater can be deadly as it induces dehydration due to its high salt content. Similarly, due to these osmotic challenges, freshwater fish are unable to survive in seawater and seawater fish face challenges in freshwater.

In cell biology, water contributes significantly to the formation of cell membranes. Every cell is formed by two layers of molecules called phospholipids. Phospholipids have two components; one is polar, and another is nonpolar. The polar component will interact with water and the nonpolar component will interact with each other and avoid water. This water selectivity allows salt and nutrients to enter and exit the cell. Because of this water interaction, cells can keep essential nutrients and salts inside, while keeping the harmful molecules at bay.

In the DNA functionality, water emerges as a key component. The shape of DNA is fundamental to its decoding abilities. One DNA can bind only with other DNA with similar shapes. Water molecules surrounded in the DNA contribute to maintaining this specific shape. Without this, cells will not be able to follow instructions decoded by DNA and pass them into future cells. This is fundamental for growth, reproduction and survival. How water plays an active role as a biomolecule is further described below.

The Biomolecule

Proteins are the building blocks of life. It is involved in countless cellular functions. Water provides a multifaceted role as a biomolecule in protein structure and catalytic chemical reactions.

Proteins are composed of amino acids and their structure is vital for proper functioning. Water is involved in the folding and stabilisation of protein structures. The hydrophobic effect of nonpolar amino acids minimises the contact with water. Hence, the water molecules surround the hydrophobic regions that stabilise the structure of proteins. Also, for maintaining protein stability, water molecules form a hydration shell around proteins and interact with the protein surface through hydrogen bonding. Similarly, the protection provided by the water shields the protein from any fluctuation in pressure and temperature which can affect its stability.

In addition to this, water actively participates in catalytic chemical reactions facilitated by proteins, known as enzymes. Water molecules act as reactants or products in enzymic reactions. In some reactions, water acts as a donor or acceptor while many other reactions, water is either added or removed. This complex involvement of water in biological processes is fundamental and adds many mysteries of life at the molecular level. That's why water is known as the "matrix of life."

The Digester

Drinking a single glass of water can significantly impact our digestion process. Water acts as a crucial facilitator for various digestive functions. Its influence is evident from the moment it enters our body, starting with its cleansing effect on the stomach and its role as a digestive aid.

Upon entering the intestine, water is swiftly absorbed. Within minutes, an equivalent amount of water is secreted into the stomach through its glandular layer in the mucosa. This process plays an important role in breaking down food during digestion, particularly in the digestion of solid foods.

Our stomach needs water in two important ways. Firstly, water is essential to produce hydrochloric acid, a vital component that aids in breaking down food. Water and carbon dioxide in the parietal cells of the stomach wall produce carbonic acid. Spontaneously, it dissociates into hydrogen and bicarbonate ions. The bicarbonate ions moved out of the cell in exchange for chloride ions. The chloride ions and hydrogen ions are transported into the stomach lumen and form hydrochloric acid. The creation of hydrochloric acid ensures an optimal pH level in the stomach for effective digestion. The fluid formed in this reaction, then moves into the intestine, establishing a natural buffer state. Below the cells, sodium bicarbonate is produced and trapped in the water layer acting as a protective barrier. This bicarbonate layer, which is alkaline in nature, prevents the acid from directly affecting the stomach tissues by neutralising it.

Secondly, water plays a crucial role in the formation of the mucus lining of the stomach. This lining is essential as it safeguards the stomach tissues from direct contact with the acid produced during digestion. Without this lining, the acid will have direct contact with stomach tissues, resulting in the development of ulcers. Also, without an adequate water supply, digestion issues may arise, leading to various difficulties such as heartburn, fatigue, and even memory loss.

The Moisturizer

How does it feel when your skin, eyes, nose, or mouth gets dry?

When we face the above situations, it indicates not only discomfort but also a signal of dehydration. It is our body's signal for water. When we consume water, it goes beyond quenching our thirst and regulating our body temperature. It ensures that our tissues are adequately moistened. Keeping our body hydrated helps it retain optimum levels of moisture, making our skin healthy and smooth.

The significance of water becomes particularly evident in skincare. Once our skin gets all the water it needs, it fights dryness, prevents premature ageing, and manages a variety of allergies and skin problems.

The Saliva

Are we Herbivorous, Carnivorous or omnivorous?

The question of our dietary nature sparked debates among many, with the widespread perception that humans are omnivorous. We can eat vegetables, plants, and animals. A closer examination of our anatomy and physiology suggests a different narrative.

Our physical characteristics give some compelling insights. Unlike carnivorous animals with sharp claws, our nails are soft, and our fingers bear no resemblance to those of meat-eating animals. Moreover, our teeth align more closely with those of herbivores, such as cows, but with the exception that we have four canine teeth. Most of our teeth are designed for cutting and grinding action and they can move front and back and side by side. Our canine teeth are not as sharp as carnivorous but manageable enough to tear into food like crunchy vegetables and soft meat. Our intestines and digestive systems are not designed for swallowing. This anatomy and physiology debate herbivorous and omnivorous nature in us. There it comes to the importance of saliva.

Our saliva is made of 99% water and the remaining one per cent consists of uric acid, electrolytes, digestive enzymes, cholesterol, and mucus-forming proteins. Our digestive process begins in the mouth with saliva. It works as a solvent for dissolving food and distributing it to taste buds. Saliva contains enzymes which split the bond of sugar molecules in the carbohydrates. This is why we get sweetness when we chew rice or potatoes for a longer time.

Saliva keeps our mouths moist. This water serves as our body's frontline defence against oral bacteria. Saliva also contains white blood cells to fight infections in wounds. Often you may notice and wonder why animals lick their wounds.

What I mentioned in this chapter is a small yet significant portion of water activities in our bodies. It is not a complete narrative, and it provides only a glimpse into the sophisticated relationship between our bodies and water. My intention is not to do a medical article with data dumping. I purposefully avoided the complex approaches where water affects our bodies.

An in-depth exploration of such a complex process forms an elaborate scientific chapter and may deviate from the reading comfort of a common person. When we delve into more scientific study, water offers a deep insight into the relationship between water and our bodily functions.

In short, when you look closely towards the water, you will be surprised to know that most major and minor functions and activities in our body are in some way or other connected to water.

Now, beyond the discussions on bodily functions, let us zoom in on one of the most remarkable components of our existence – the brain.

Chapter 4

Brainstorming

"Water is probably the most studied and least understood".

— Felix Franks

In a South Asian country, a few scientists and defence authorities gathered to discuss the development of a biological weapon for mass destruction. The meeting is held in a secret location. This meeting was aimed at brainstorming the weapon's properties and destructive capabilities. However, an unexpected turn of events disrupted the proceedings.

Midway through the meeting, a sense of discomfort swept through the room, leading to some losing consciousness. All personnel who attended the meeting were promptly transported to the hospital and they were diagnosed with severe food poisoning. However, they consumed only water provided during the meeting. Doctors suspected water poisoning, but the extensive test failed to reveal any toxic substance in the water. Water was suitable for drinking.

The mystery surrounding the scientist's poisoning prompted a thorough investigation. Years later, the investigation concluded that the scientists had been poisoned by the very ordinary water they drank during the meeting. The strange toxicity of the seemingly harmless water added another layer to the mystery till today.

Our brain is the most complex structure known in the universe. Comprising 80% of water, the adult human brain weighs around 1.5 Kilograms, consisting of only 1/50th of our body weight. Despite its relatively small size, the brain is a hungry consumer. The brain utilises 25% of the body's oxygen, and nutrients, and 70% of its glucose level. In addition to water, the brain comprises fatty acids, proteins, carbohydrates, and a variety of salts.

Neurons are our information messengers, generally called nerve cells. Neurons process and transmit information through electrical and chemical signals. These signals between neurons occur via synapses. Synapses are specialized contact between neurons where information is passed from one neuron to the next. Neurons can connect to form neural networks. These networks are the core components of our nervous system.

The nervous system is controlled by our brain. Remarkably, the brains organise a hundred billion neuron signals, known as neurotransmitters, fostering communication. With a stunning thousand trillion synaptic connections, the brain continually receives and processes sensory information. Let us look into the role of water in brain function.

Water plays a crucial role in supplying essential electrical energy to our brains. Water ensures the brain's optimum functionality, including thought and memory processes. According to Dr Corinne Allen, visionary founder of the Advanced Learning and Development Institute, brain cells need two times more energy than other cells in the body. Water provides this energy.

Our brain is the centre of cognitive function and provides us with the power to think, plan, speak, dream, memorise, reason, and experience emotions. When our brain is operated with a well-hydrated, full reserve of water, it enhances our cognitive abilities. We will be able to think faster, be more focused, and experience greater clarity and creativity.

Our brain cells completely depend on water to carry out many essential functions. One of the main things is our ability to perform the mental process that allows us to understand and relate to the world effectively. We constantly use this function, and our brains work harder to accomplish the task. Many recent studies concluded that the performance of cognitive tasks is dependent on the water level in our brains. Shortage of water can have a negative impact on the brain. When our brain lacks sufficient water, it accelerates cognitive decline and prolonged water shortage leads to dementia-like situations.

There is wonderful engineering, and the technological mechanism is in our brain which mastered the water distribution and control cycle in our body. Let's look into the role of the hypothalamus and pituitary gland to understand this process better.

The hypothalamus is situated beneath the brain, and the pituitary gland is located below the hypothalamus. These are remarkably complex structures with multilayered roles. The main function of the hypothalamus is to keep our body in a stable condition called homeostasis. The hypothalamus governs various bodily functions such as body temperature, digestion, blood pressure, heart rate, respiration, sleep cycle and so on. However, we will focus especially on the relationship with water regulations.

Our body has eight major glands, and all are interrelated. The pituitary gland is the most important gland in our body. They produce certain hormones and coordinate the activities of other glands. It also directs them to release their hormones. Since it has mastery over other glands, it's often referred to as the master gland. The hypothalamus and pituitary gland work like a bridge. The hypothalamus directs commands to the pituitary gland, which, in turn, generates hormones. These hormones then traverse to the bloodstream, conveying instructions to various organs and glands.

Osmosis, as mentioned in an earlier chapter is the maintenance of equilibrium in the body. Electrolytes, the body minerals are spread throughout our body and most essential for various cellular functioning and performance. Inside the hypothalamus, there are special cells called osmoreceptors. These cells monitor the water and electrolyte levels.

When our body has enough water, the osmoreceptors also have the right amount of water. But, if there is a water shortage, osmoreceptors shrink and send signals to pituitary glands. This gland will release a hormone called anti-diuretic hormone which directs kidneys to preserve water and not urinate.

Similarly, if there is too much water, the osmoreceptors swell and this prompts the kidney to release more water. This phenomenon of water management is called osmoregulation. This process is happening not only in the hypothalamus but also in the kidneys and bloodstream. When we sweat or bleed or indulge in activities which affect the body temperature and body pressure, osmoregulation takes place.

Our brains rely on adequate hydration for optimal functioning. Brain cells need a precise balance of water and various elements to work effectively. Sufficient water ensures a harmonious operation, while inadequate hydration disrupts the balance and brain cells lose efficiency. When the water supply is less than our brain's requirements, we are in trouble.

White matter and grey matter are the essential part of our brain. Grey matter constitutes 40% of our brain and white matter constitutes the remaining 60%. Grey matter is a type of tissue that plays a crucial role in our day-to-day functions. It serves as the seat for thinking and reasoning, where information processing occurs. Meanwhile, white matter facilitates the communication between grey matter areas and the rest of the body.

Grey matter begins forming during the foetal stage and continues to increase its volume until around the age of eight. However, the density of grey matter continues to grow until around the age of 20. This process is the basis of our mental development. Insufficient water intake can lead to the shrinkage of grey matter in size and mass. This can cause premature ageing of the brain and neuron damage. Damaged neurons cannot be replaced. As a natural part of our growing process, we require to have enough water to assist the growth of grey matter. As we get older, our ability to recognise thirst will decline, increasing the risk and its detrimental effects on the brain.

Understanding the inner workings of our brain with water is very insightful and beneficial for our well-being. Also, examining the details of our cell structure further emphasises the critical role of water. Some details regarding the relationship between water and cells are discussed previously.

In cell biology, there are two key fluid compartments: the intracellular fluid, generally known as ICF and the extracellular fluid, known as ECF. ICF is the fluid within the cells and the ECF is outside the cells. Water is distributed between these compartments, with ICF holding approximately 65% of body water and ECF containing the remaining 35%. Apart from water, essential minerals such as chloride, potassium and sodium are vital for maintaining the ICF and ECF levels.

The process of ICF and ECF is governed by hormonal messages from the brain and kidneys. When water levels decrease, mineral molecules will concentrate, prompting the transfer of water from one compartment to another compartment for dilution. Our cell sensors detect this process and signal the brain about the lack of water or cell dehydration. In response, the brain instructs the body to drink more water.

Whenever minerals or salts become too concentrated, the brain will signal the body to drink more water until the balance is restored. This meticulous process is critical for maintaining the body's internal environment. In many Indian languages, the proverb "One who eats salt must drink water sooner or later" is for gauging the integrity and character of a person and is colloquially associated with this process.

Every function of our brain is monitored, measured, and influenced by the efficient flow of water. Multiple studies pointed out that our mental health and happiness index relates to hydration. Optimal hydration is essential for the brain to produce dopamine and serotonin. Dopamine, known as the "happy hormone," contributes to the feeling of happiness, motivation, alertness, and focus. Insufficient dopamine levels can create fatigue, sadness, lack of motivation, memory loss, mood swings, sleep issues, concentration problems, and reduced sex drive.

Serotonin production is one of the most complex systems in our brains. Optimal hydration allows the brain to make more serotonin. Serotonin facilitates the communication between the brain and the body. These messages tell our bodies how to work. Known as a "feel-good" chemical, adequate serotonin levels, make us focused happier, and calmer. Low levels of serotonin result in depression, digestive issues, suicidal thoughts, and panic disorders.

The decreased water level in the brain cells also causes proteins to misfold, preventing the clearance of toxic proteins. Sooner, these toxic proteins build up in the brain resulting in various impairments. Many hypotheses suggest that water shortage in the brain will lead to a decrease in brain volume, an increase in the ventricular volume, and an increase in cortex thickness. When the brain starts shrinking, it can lead to problems associated with thinking, memory, and performing everyday tasks. Water supports the brain's ability to function optimally, keeping our mental processes sharp and effective. Drinking enough water is a major way to boost our brain power.

Thirst is a clear signal for dehydration. When dehydrated, we have difficulty keeping our attention focused. Even a one percentage dehydration level results in a five-percentage reduction in cognitive function. A two-percentage drop in body water leads to short-term memory loss and difficulty in concentrating. As we lose more water from our brains, an additional complication arises.

Dehydration is a simple but complex condition that can lead to severe physical and mental complications and even death. We'll explore dehydration from a common man's perspective in the next chapter.

Chapter 5

Dehydration – Physical and Mental

'It is chronic dehydration that is the root cause of most major diseases.'

– Dr. F. Batmanghelidj, M.D

What keeps us alive?

We are alive because we breathe in and breathe out. We are alive because, just like water circulates in the earth to sustain life, it circulates throughout our body for our survival.

What will happen when we don't have enough water in our bodies?

Water is the second most vital substance for our survival after air. But often our medical systems show a lack of attention to this, or their focus is limited to molecular and biological aspects. Essentially, every bodily function depends on the efficient flow of water. Dehydration, the condition arising from an inefficient water intake, is a critical concern.

Adequate water in our body signifies hydration - a preventive measure and a simple physiological cure for many deceases.

When we are dehydrated, the water metabolism of the body is disturbed and compromised. It triggers a variety of signals that prompt chemical and physical regulatory actions in the brain. The brain will activate the neurotransmitter system which results in the production of histamine, and other subordinate agents to ration the water. Once histamine activities happen in our body, we start feeling thirsty. Severe dehydration is accompanied by a pain called dyspeptic pain.

Dehydration will start when we lose about one to two per cent of water. This will lead to thirst and a decline in physical and mental performance. Prolonged dehydration impacts our short-term and long-term memory. Our ability to perform simple arithmetic calculations and analytical power is compromised. Extended dehydration causes brain cells to shrink. Symptoms such as depression, anger, emotional instability, stress, sleep deprivation, and lack of mental clarity are the result of extended dehydration. A water loss of about 4 to 5 per cent brings about more severe symptoms like fatigue, loss of appetite, headaches, and dizziness. If the body water loss is more than 5%, the risk increases, possibly leading to life-threatening consequences.

Thirst is not the first indicator of the body's need for water. By the time, we feel thirsty, considerable water loss is already occurred. Our body has initiated the water regulation process. Waiting for thirst before hydrating can have long-term detrimental effects. The root cause of many degenerative deceases is not fully understood even today. We blame it on genetics, lifestyle changes and other cogenerated situations. Consistent water intake can prevent many degenerative deceases to a greater extent.

At different stages of life, our bodies exhibit varying compositions, comprising 65 to 90% water and 10 to 35% solids. Our body is dynamically designed to do water regulation from birth till death. As mentioned earlier, water management unfolds in three stages - the foetus stage, the growth stage, and the life stage.

During the foetus stage, which occurs within the mother's uterus, the necessary water for cell growth and other functions will be provided by the mother. When a cell begets its progeny, over 75% of its volume comprises water. The availability of water significantly influences foetal growth. The water intake decision rests with foetal tissues, but its impact resonates with the mother.

Many scientists hypothesise that morning sickness during pregnancy may be the foetus and mother's signal for thirst, underlining the importance of proper water intake. Prolonged morning sickness can potentially affect the foetus and proper hydration is very much essential during pregnancy.

As we move into the growth stage, all developmental processes unfold, and the body continues to regulate and adjust the water content. Once we reach adulthood, the body's water content stabilises at around 70%, gradually decreasing to approximately 65% in later stages. Often older individuals have 3-5% less water content in their bodies compared to their younger generations.

Ensuring regular water intake is important for preventing dehydration. A dry mouth is the second syndrome, after thirst, which indicates serious dehydration. A dry mouth is a critical sign of dehydration. However, our body can suffer from dehydration even when the mouth is moist. But, for elderly people, it can happen due to various other reasons too.

When we have a dry mouth, we begin experiencing speech deprivation, difficulty in tasting food and many times a dry throat. Dehydration is one of the reasons that significantly affects saliva production. When our digestive system is in water conservation mode, it can halt saliva production.

Dyspeptic pain is an advanced signal of acute dehydration. Once we have persistent dyspeptic pain, major diseases will start appearing in the body. The mucus barrier in the stomach is our natural protective shield against any acid and its efficiency depends on regular water intake. Ingested food will stimulate acid production and the mucus barrier provides natural protection. Any disturbance can lead to dyspeptic pain, eventually leading to conditions like heartburn, ulcers, and gastritis complications in the body.

Chronic dyspeptic pain due to dehydration can contribute to a range of health issues like bad temper and it can also be associated with some of the major illnesses including allergies, asthma, and other degenerative diseases. For the digestion of food, water is the most essential ingredient and once we give enough water to the body before food, we can control the cholesterol formation in the blood vessel to some extent.

Joint and back pain is often related to dehydration. Water acts as a lubricating agent for our joints. In most joints, an intermittent vacuum promotes water circulation, and when we move, the pressure squeezes the water within the joints. The hydraulic properties of water stores in the disc core are essential for all joint movements.

The spinal joints and disc structures rely heavily on the water stored in the disc core. This water not only lubricates the contact surface of the joints but also supports the weight of the upper body. Almost 75% of the weight of our upper body is supported by the water stored in the disc core. To maintain this support system, it is crucial to ensure we drink enough water. Dehydration is a significant factor in 60% of general back pain cases.

In a stressful situation, it's common advice to take deep breaths and drink water. We often wondered about the relationship between water, stress, and depression. Previous discussions have highlighted the role of dopamine and serotonin concerning water. Ongoing studies explore the connection between water and social stress associated with fear, anxiety, insecurity, and emotional problems.

Some studies suggest that depression arising from social stress may result from a deficiency of water in the brain. Our brain relies on the electrical energy generated by the water. When we become dehydrated, the brain's energy generation decreases. Hence, functions of the brain that depend on this electrical energy become inefficient. This inefficiency leads us to a depressive state and puts us in a series of physiological problems associated with social stress.

Is dehydration the culprit behind hypertension? This question sparks debates, with various opinions. Let us examine further. Blood pressure is a measure of the force exerted by the heart to circulate blood, typically measured with a range of 80-120 mmHg. Any deviation from this range causes hypertension. Hypertension can be due to various reasons, and it is often called a lifestyle disorder.

Sometimes, hypertension is linked to dehydration. Inadequate water intake can lead to cellular dehydration. Due to this, capillary beds in less active areas of the body will have to shut to adjust to the dehydrated situation. This selective closure is a balancing effect. If chronic dehydration is continued for a prolonged period, water metabolism in our body is disturbed. Studies found that this can be a major reason for hypertension.

Water is the cheapest medicine for us. Dehydration will produce many major diseases. Studies even connect Alzheimer's disease to brain cell dehydration. Regular attention to water intake can significantly prevent various illnesses.

In the words of Dr Willian Grey, *"There is more natural magic in a glass full of water than any medication"*.

In the upcoming chapter, we will delve into the role of water in medicinal systems.

Chapter 6

Medicinal Water

"A man's health cannot be borne even in the best-stocked pharmacy "

— Aldous Huxley

The etymology of the term "water" traces its origin to the Sanskrit word *"Apah"*, which means "Animate "or "something that gives life". As the name indicates, water is used as medicine for healing, curing, therapy, and rehabilitation. This practice is an ancient and revered science.

In Persian culture, the word *"ab"* carries the meaning of water. *Abad* and *Abadi* are derived from the word *ab*. *Abad* means prosperous and *Abadi* means flourishing, both translated to a civilised society. The word *abad* is also widely used in Arabic and Urdu culture with profound meaning showcasing the eternal nature of water. Many Indian cities like Ahmedabad, Hyderabad and Islamabad city in Pakistan are named considering these aspects.

Every civilization adopted a water-based cure for treating many illnesses and disorders. Eastern medicinal systems always take a holistic approach to health. Traditional Asian healthcare practitioners considered the interconnectedness of body, mind, and spirit (soul). They look into the body, and emotional health to understand what is going on in someone's life.

Ayurveda, the science of life, traces its origin back to the ancient Indus Valley Civilization. As per Hinduism, Dhanvantari is hailed as the "Father of Ayurveda". Vedas are the fundamental scriptures of Hindu philosophy and provide the earliest glimpse into the principles of Ayurveda. Sushruta and Charaka, distinguished teachers of ancient times, made profound contributions to Ayurveda. Sushruta is acclaimed as the "Father of Surgery", and Charaka is revered as the "Father of Indian Medicine". *Sushruta Samhita* and *Charaka Samhita* are the two main sets of texts that form the foundation of Ayurvedic medicinal practices.

Ayurveda is a holistic approach that integrates the physical, psychological, and spiritual facets of an individual's well-being. The foundational principles of Ayurveda revolve around the concept of *panchabhuta*, representing the five great elements: earth, water, air, fire, and space. These elements form the fundamental building block of the human body. Ayurveda further defines these five elemental combinations into three constitutions, *Prakriti*, called *Vata, Pitha* and *Kapha*.

Every human body comprises a unique blend of these three constitutions and any deviation from their harmonious balance can lead to the emergence of *doshas*, loosely translated as "that which can cause problems". *Doshas* are responsible for our well-being and imbalanced *doshas* will result in poor health. *Vata* consisting of air and space, *Pitha* comprising fire and water and *kabha* consisting of earth and water, collectively shape our personality, characteristics, strengths, and weaknesses.

Ayurveda suggests that recognising the individual ratio of these *doshas* is crucial, as it forms the basis of personalised medicinal approaches. Balancing these *doshas* is the way to a person's overall well-being. Ayurvedic treatments are tailored to restore this equilibrium, using a combination of curative and preventive measures.

Water plays a fundamental role in Ayurvedic treatment. Within Ayurvedic principles, water is associated with lunar energy. In Ayurveda, water is revered as the body's guardian, with six essential qualities: *Jivana* means the quality of enlivening, *Tarpana*, the quality of satiating, *Hrudya* the quality of heartiness, *Hlaadi*, the quality of mindfulness, *Buddhiprasobhana*, the quality of stimulating mind and *Mrushta,* the quality of Pure.

Ayurveda expresses the significance of water in the human body through five distinct ways. Firstly, salivary fluid, equipped with salivary amylase, protects the mouth against damage during chewing. Secondly, water safeguards the stomach's mucous membranes from acid harm. The third dimension involves joint moisturisation, while the fourth ensures respiratory system protection. Finally, the maintenance of mucous membranes in the lungs. Based on these insights, ayurveda harnesses water's varied qualities to address various health conditions and many Ayurvedic formulations are aligned with this conceptual understanding.

Medicated water is widely explained in many Ayurvedic texts. It is an innovative mode of medication for physical and mental well-being and enhances longevity. Ayurveda has a very detailed description of various properties, types, purification, indication and utilization of water in our daily life. It also specifies various therapeutic uses of water. Water can be used as supplementary to primary medication or a standalone remedy for many health problems.

Traditional Ayurvedic wisdom emphasizes a prescribed rule for water intake for maintaining physical and mental strength and life span. The detailed descriptions cover water's properties, purification methods, types, indications, and daily life applications. This perspective is outlined in later chapters.

Traditional Chinese medicine (TCM) follows a similar vein to Ayurveda, placing significant emphasis on the interconnectedness of the five elements and their impact on our lives. However, the great elements considered in TCM are a little different from Ayurveda, recognising Wood, Fire, Earth, Metal and Water. These elements are not static, but are in constant movement, undergoing continuous changes by the natural cycles and the passage of time.

At the core of TCM philosophy is the concept of "*qi*", the life force energy that flows through these five elements. Their dynamic interplay holds a great influence on our well-being, with the ebb and flow affecting our health. These elements are closely associated with our organs, senses, and emotions.

As per TCM, each element governs specific bodily systems. Wood governs the liver and gallbladder, Fire presides over the heart, Earth regulates the stomach, Metal guides the lungs and Water governs the kidneys.

A state of optimal health is characterised by the harmonious and free flow of "*qi*" through these elements. Any imbalance or disturbances in this flow lead to various health issues. The objective of TCM practices is to restore and preserve this delicate balance, ensuring the optimal functioning of the body and mind.

When we examine the Western medicinal system, water is seen as a powerful tool of healing, an alternative therapy. The usage of water for cure is well demonstrated and widely used by the ancient Romans, Egyptians, and Greeks.

The ancient Greeks were big believers in the healing properties of water. They have a religious significance with water and believe that the water has a mystical and medicinal power. The Romans initially took cues from the Greeks in their medicinal system. However, they developed their own sophisticated system in the later stages. The ancient Egyptians also had sophisticated systems of using water for medicinal purposes. They had some advanced techniques, combining water with natural and herbal remedies to treat various elements.

Over millennia, different cultures around the world developed their own ways of using water for healing. A kind of universal remedy that stood the test of time. This historical significance of water as a healing aliment transcends time and continues to play a vital role in modern approaches to medicine. Hydrotherapy is one such development that takes place in the later stages.

Vincenz Priessnitz, born in 1799 in the Austrian village of Grafenberg, emerged from a humble beginning in a poor farming family. Raised in poverty, he took up farming early in life due to his father's blindness and the death of his elder brother. During his adolescence, he observed a wounded deer healing its injured limp by immersing it in pond water. Inspired by this, he successfully applied this method to cure his injured finger wounded during timber chopping.

At the age of 17, Priessnitz faced a severe accident where a horsecart's wheel ran over him, resulting in broken ribs. Despite doctors expressing doubt about his recovery, Priessnitz was confident about his treatment method. He continued his method of wet bandages and consuming spring water and managed to heal himself within a year.

Determined to share his newfound knowledge, Priessnitz developed a systematic approach to cold water therapy. Starting in his village, he expanded his healing practices to treat humans and animals. His practices gained widespread recognition. Also, he faced opposition and legal challenges from traditional doctors. However, Priessnitz consistently demonstrated the effectiveness of his water-healing approach in various courts in Austria.

In 1826, Priessnitz earned royal recognition by treating the emperor's family, significantly boosting acceptance of his water therapy across Austria and Europe. In 1845, he received the highest civilian award in Vienna, from Archduke Franz Carl. Later, Priessnitz's influence extended beyond Europe, reaching various parts of America. Numerous hydropathic medical schools and journals dedicated to his method emerged. Over 400 books were published on hydrotherapy based on his teachings.

Vincenz Priessnitz passed away in 1851, and a museum in Lazne Jesenik, Czech Republic, was named in his honour, marking the site of the first hydropathy institute. In 1911, Vienna unveiled a statue in tribute to him and a foundation in Poland named after him. UNESCO also recognises his birth anniversary as an important milestone in history, acknowledging his significant contribution to the world.

Vincenz Preessnitz is acknowledged as the father of modern hydrotherapy. According to his philosophy, good health comes from the body's ability to overcome challenges. As per him, illness results from bad fluids and substances in the body. Bad fluids are the results of disordered lifestyles and bad substances are from foreign elements. He believes medicines are foreign to the body and chooses an animal's way of treating diseases with human intelligence. Priessnitz treated over 40,000 patients using cold water, fresh air, systematic body movement and healthy food, without relying on medicines.

In his view, cold water prompts the body to produce its own heat, strengthening its defence and expelling harmful substances. He emphasises that the healing power lies not only in the cold water but also in the energy it stimulates.

As per the hydropathic philosophies by Priessnitz, life is one of the expressions of energy. More energy, more life in it. He believes that the illness accumulates gradually, and the stimulation of energy is not a quick fix. Hydrotherapy also has its limitations, and it is not a miraculous elixir of life. However, with water, time, movement, and moderation, it can effectively address a spectrum of ailments.

While Vincenz Priessnitz's hydrotherapy had its limitations, his global recognition attests to the effectiveness of his approach, earning him the title of the "Father of Modern Hydrotherapy" and "Columbus of Medicine".

Sebastian Kneipp, a German Catholic priest developed another form of hydrotherapy called "Kneippism". Kneippism is based on the theory that all diseases originate in the circulatory system of the body. He followed Vincenz Priessnitz 's footsteps initially, but later, delved into a distinctive version of the treatment. He infused holistic and spiritual dimensions to the treatment.

Kneipp's distinctive approach incorporated the use of cold water, herbs and prayers with a belief that remedies were fundamentally provided by a divine force. Kneipp documented his methods and beliefs in the widely acclaimed book "My Water Cure", a 19th-century bestseller translated into numerous languages.

In 1891, Kneipp established the Kneipp Fund, dedicated to promoting water healing, a legacy that endures to this day. This visionary initiative paved the way for the establishment of Kneipp societies in the Americas. Over time, these societies are evolved and eventually renamed "The Naturopathic Society of America". Today, Kneippism has become an integral part of mainstream medicine in Germany and various European nations.

Balneology is the scientific exploration of the therapeutic properties of natural thermal water. The basic roots of balneology are established in both Western and Eastern traditions. The healing effects of thermal water have been harnessed for centuries to address a spectrum of health issues ranging from inflammation to dermatitis to rheumatological, musculoskeletal and chronic skin conditions. The versatile application of natural or medicinal thermal water involves bathing, inhaling, drinking and body packing.

Among the history of balneology, sulphur water stands out as one of its oldest forms. Locations such as hot springs, blue lagoons, and the Dead Sea have served as bastions for balneological practices for centuries. The balneology-based spa therapy is gaining popularity nowadays due to its systematic use of minerals, controlled temperature, and the healing power of water.

Watsu, a formative aquatic technique with warm water, echo the human body's natural temperature. This practice, conceived by Harold Dull in 1980, goes beyond conventional physical therapies. *Watsu* represents a harmonious fusion of movement, massage, and water immersion, with a primary focus on the holistic well-being of both the body and the mind.

Cryotherapy emerges as a pioneering alternative to surgical interventions across diverse tissues in our bodies. It is a method that harnesses the power of water at exceptionally low temperatures to obliterate diseased tissues. Its versatility in addressing skin disorders and muscular strains, making it a favoured choice among athletes grappling with injuries such as sprains and soft tissue damage.

Rooted in 19th-century France, *Thalassotherapy* is an integration of seawater's healing properties into wellness practices. The popularity of this approach is demonstrated in saltwater public baths scattered across many European countries. The therapeutic potential of seawater, supplemented with minerals and elements, forms the foundation of *Thalassotherapy.*

Hydrotherapy has been used widely in animals for many centuries. Seawater immersion of horses for healing injuries is practised in many parts of the world. In the same context, canine hydrotherapy has gained acclaim among dog owners seeking solutions for an array of health conditions for their pets.

Cold plunge has recently emerged as a new trend for therapeutic practice for both the body and the mind. Cold plunging involves submerging the body in cold water preferably below 15 degrees Celsius for a specific period. It is an age-old practice which provides physiological and psychological benefits such as blood circulation improvement, muscle strain reduction, immunity enhancement, mood-boosting, mental awareness, and various other benefits for the body, skin and hair.

Many times, water often challenges established scientific paradigms. The best-known fact is about homoeopathy. Many homoeopathic remedies leverage water for dilutions, prompting ongoing debates about the mechanism of action underlying their efficacy. Homeopathy has garnered widespread acceptance worldwide, functioning as a prominent alternative medicinal approach. This unconventional yet effective practice was discussed in detail in this book.

Water therapy or hydrotherapy is an age-old practice deeply rooted in various civilizations. As we delve into historical records, a narrative unfolds across the periods, revealing the utilisation of hydrotherapy in the cultures of Egypt, Persia, Greece, Asia, Africa and Rome. Native Americans and South Americans have a variety of water-based holistic therapies for curing the illness.

Some use movements and exercises, others adjust their temperature for healing effects, and some apply compressed water to specific body areas. Submerging in water is also a therapeutic approach. Additionally, these methods often incorporate elements like medicinal herbs, rock salt, epsom salts, nutrients, mud, clay aromatic oils, minerals, and leaves.

Water as medicine has had a significant role in human wellness for centuries. However, in the 18th and 19th centuries and even after that, diseases like cholera, tuberculosis, pneumonia, jaundice, smallpox, and various bacterial and virus infections accounted for about 70% of global deaths.

Water therapy and natural therapy had limited success in treating these communicable diseases and were taken backstage. An urgent need for solutions, complemented by scientific advancement, led to the emergence of modern allopathic medicines. This modern medicinal system played a crucial role in developing medicines and vaccines for both treatment and prevention. By the 20th century, many communicable diseases were either eradicated or effectively controlled through advancements in allopathic medicine.

However, the 21ˢᵗ century presents a different health challenge. Today, the world is grappling with a significant rise in lifestyle-related deceases such as diabetes, cancer, hypertension, high cholesterol, anxiety, depression and other lifestyle-related complications. These complications collectively contribute to two-thirds of the recent deaths. This shift in disease patterns has prompted a new perspective in the field of health and overall well-being.

In the modern era, there is growing recognition of the preventive benefits of hydropathy, naturopathy, and water therapy in managing and preventing lifestyle-related diseases. Today, hydropathic, and naturopathic health tourism have become popular in various parts of the world. Water, in its various forms, emerges as a powerful element for healing. The focus is now on holistic approaches that combine traditional and alternative therapies, acknowledging the signified role water plays in promoting health and wellbeing.

I have dedicated several chapters to help you to grasp the sophisticated relationship between our bodies and water. While some information may be familiar, I aim to present a comprehensive understanding. As each organ functions as a water container, water plays a crucial role in every bodily function, surpassing the conventional perception as a typical liquid.

Water behaves uniquely as a liquid, drawing various perspectives from science, culture, religion, and philosophy. Regardless of viewpoint, there is a consensus about water's special nature. It is not just about its impact on bodily functions; water extends its influence on our thoughts, actions, emotions, responses, moods, and more. Recognising this, we can leverage water to attain physical, mental, and energy balance.

Our ancestors believed that life hinged on water's peculiar behaviour. So, while you have traversed the familiar territory of bodily functions, there is a vast and fascinating world within water waiting to be explored. Understanding this allows us to use water judiciously to achieve our desired balance. The more delve into this topic, the clearer its significance becomes.

Chapter 7

A Different Perspective

*"If you put water into a cup, it becomes the cup.
You put water into a bottle, and it becomes the bottle.
You put it in a teapot it becomes the teapot.*

*Now, water can flow, or it can crash.
Be water, my friend.".*

— *Bruce Lee*

Nathan Zohner, a 14-year-old student at Eagle Rock Junior High School in Bonneville County, USA, made a lasting impact with his 1997 science project named "How Gullible Are We". His interesting project was all about banning a chemical called dihydrogen monoxide or DHMO. He presented his petition to his classmates advocating for the ban of DHMO.

Zohner's project had a detailed report explaining the dangers of DHMO, alleging its involvement in thousands of annual deaths. His report highlighted the presence of DHMO in tumours and cancer cells and underlined that prolonged use of DHMO can cause excessive sweating, high urination, nausea, omitting, and disturbing the electrolyte balances in the body. Zohner went on to claim that DHMO could cause serious burns in a gaseous state, triggering corrosion of metals, and mineral escapes from natural landscapes contributing to the greenhouse gas effects.

His reports assert that DHMO has been found in lakes, and rivers, which caused millions of dollars of property damages. Zohner emphasised that DHMO is difficult to remove even after washing and dumping into the rivers and streams which is creating pollution, health hazards, and environmental impacts. His reports revealed that the government is refusing to ban DHMO, instead, they are extensively using DHMO in the military and developing technologies to use in a warfare situation.

Not surprisingly, when Zohner conducted a vote among his classmates, 43 out of 50 students favoured banning DHMO, six were undecided but not objected. Only one student recognized the true nature of Zohner's puzzling project and objected to it. After the voting, Zohner revealed the true identity of DHMO. It was water, H2O, which can also be represented as Dihydrogen Monoxide or DHMO.

His project was a clear experiment to expose the "gullibility" of people. Zohner's paradoxical project gained considerable attention from the media. Journalist James K Glassman coined the term *"Zohnerism"* to describe the intentional distortion of facts to draw unrelated and false conclusions.

"Zohnerism" has since become a common phenomenon, influencing our understanding of various issues. We get the information in a particular way which can mislead us to draw wrong conclusions. It can be the basis of shaping our understanding of most issues. *Zohnerism* is widely spread in our daily lives as we come across it through newspapers, social media, the internet, magazines, journals, and word of mouth. We are often the victim of this and make our conclusions based on this false information. Water, from the beginning, became a victim of *"Zohnerism."*

Many times, our understanding of water has been overshadowed by the misinformation and conspiracies spanning over centuries. Our ancient history has many records of the harmonious and respected existence between water and humans. Irrespective of our faith, nationality, country and region, water was held in high esteem, surrounded by respect and devotion. Unfortunately, this sentiment seems to be diminishing.

During our scientific revolution era since the 15th century, we have had substantial technological and industrial advancements across various fields, However, except in the medicinal and hydrological field, water remained overlooked in mainstream research. Its understanding was confined to daily use and religious ceremonies. Even the study of the physicochemical properties of water was not understood until the 18th century, and the chemical formula of H_2O was unknown.

One of the significant reasons may be due to the religious and cultural importance given to water. Due to this, scientists may not be interested in exploring various dimensions of water as it may invite anger from religious bodies if they present something contradictory to the current belief.

It was in 1766, when Henry Cavendish, a British physicist and chemist published a paper regarding his finding, shedding light on water's properties through his experiments with air and oxygen. He observed the formation of liquid substances and concluded that water is not an element but a compound with oxygen and inflammable air.

In 1873, Antoine Laurent Lavoisier, a French chemist reproduced Cavendish's experiment and obtained water. Around the same time, Joseph Priestley, an English chemist conducted a similar experiment by sparkling ordinary air with inflammable air in a closed vessel. This experiment also resulted in the formation of "dew" on the glass walls. Antoine Laurent Lavoisier gave the inflammable air name Hydrogen from the Greek words "hydro" and "genes" which together means 'water forming". Finally, in 1811, Amedeo Avogadro uncovered the H_2O formula of water.

Curiously, research on the water was again neglected to a greater extent till the first half of the 20th century. However, after the Second World War, scientific research in water grew. The first controversial event during this time was polywater by Russian scientist Nokole Fedyakin. He discovered that water could become unexpectedly stable in certain conditions.

Water in this condition is difficult to freeze or vaporize and has higher density and viscosity than ordinary water.

Fedyakin shared his findings with Boris Derjaguin, a famous chemist and he started further research on this peculiar water phenomenon. Using narrow capillary tubes, he found that water displayed interfacial properties when it interacted with surfaces.

This was the period that coincided with Cold War tension between the USA and the Soviet Union (USSR). The USA and their Western alliance were anxious about the technological gap between them and the USSR mainly due to the first artificial satellite launch, Sputnik, by the USSR. The publicization of Boris Derjaguin's finding made many controversial theories about the possible destruction of water sources by the USSR. There were fears that releasing this kind of water could trigger the crystallization and polymerization of the earth's water, thus making it unfit for consumption.

Many scientists from both sides joined in the experimentation and investigation, sparking a major controversy. Some experiments found that polywater contained traces of bacteria and other contaminants. What began as a scientific exploration sooner turned into a political divide and finally, it has become an experimental goof from both sides due to the Cold War effect. Even public experiments conducted by Boris Derjaguin failed due to contaminants in the water.

However, it was common knowledge that getting purified water is a near impossible task as water naturally contains traces other than water molecules. Anything in contact with water or surrounding forms and interface influences the water's composition.

The controversies surrounding Polywater gradually subsidised over time. However, scientific communities are divided largely into the following decades and the perception of water is changed based on their mindsets and malicious intentions. Presently, the water memory concept ignited a new controversy. Many scientists are engaged in a heated debate, with one side persistently opposing with other. The fourth phase of water becomes another focal point of debate. Instead of adopting a comprehensive and collective approach, these opposing sides have been locked in prolonged conflicts for decades. This discord has significantly limited the understanding of water. Water finds itself middling with controversies and subjected to *"Zohnerism."*

When we examine the diverse world of our medicinal system such as Naturopathy, Homoeopathy, Ayurveda, Unani, Traditional Chinese, and Japanese medicinal systems, we can find a common thread. They all used the therapeutic power of water to treat diseases and disorders. For example, as explained earlier, homoeopathy uses the memory of water to a certain extent for the formulations through repeated dilution of substances in the water, resulting in another mixture which contains only negligible or no traces of the original substance. However, water retains the information and produces a therapeutic effect. It is commonly expressed as "like cures like".

Despite Homoeopathy's historical success in treating millions of patients, a certain fraction of modern science is describing homoeopathy as "witchcraft". India alone hosts more than 10,000 homoeopathic hospitals and dispensaries and as per the 2021 statistics, more than 3,00,000 qualified doctors are practicing homeopathy in India. According to the National Institute of Health, more than 6 million people in the USA use homoeopathic medicine to treat specific health conditions and more than 200 million people use homoeopathy worldwide. In most countries, homoeopathy is a recognized medicinal practice and is taught in universities and medical colleges. However certain fractions of the traditional scientific community still consider homeopathy as "pseudoscience". The same is the case with other alternative medicines such as naturopathy, ayurveda, hydropathy, Unani, and Chinese and Eastern medicines. These medicinal systems bear the categorisation of "protoscience" and "parascience" by some philosophers and certain conventional scientific communities.

In my view, as I mentioned in the preface of this book, we need larger perspectives to understand water. Water requires a broader insight beyond its physiological characteristics. As you go through the various chapters, you have understood certain properties and anomalies of the water which still lack reasons and explanations. As per the latest findings, water has more than 60 anomalies which is no match with any other substance found around us.

When we closely observe these anomalies and the behaviour of water, five major observations become apparent. Firstly, water possesses the ability to collect and store information. Secondly, water can reorganise and rearrange itself in response to encountered conditions. Thirdly, water exhibits enigmatic behaviour about energy, temperature, and density. The fourth observation pertains to a state beyond solid, liquid, and gas and finally, the interplay involving geometry, hydrogen bonding and dielectric mode.

Considering various anomalies and qualities, it becomes evident that water exhibits a mysterious adaptability in its nature. Water behaves consciously, displaying an awareness of its existence. Water is always adjusting its nature to align with its surroundings.

I can provide some more information regarding the above concept to give more light on your understanding and interplay of the anomalies of water which can influence life.

Quantum physics is the study of matter and energy at a very fundamental level, meaning beyond the molecular level. This study aims to uncover the properties and behaviour of the building blocks of nature. It studies tiny objects like atoms, electrons, protons and even beyond that structure to understand the quantum phenomena in nature and around us. This scientific pursuit has given many groundbreaking inventions like Laser, MRI, microchips, and electronic microscopes.

As per the quantum theory, we are nothing, but a 20-watt fountain of energy connected with the fabric of the universe. This connection is routed in the surest axioms of science - that energy never dies; it can neither be created nor destroyed. It can only transform from one form to another form.

As per quantum physics, everything is energy that vibrates at certain frequencies. Humans, animals, metals, and plants are vibrating every moment. The whole universe is in a vibrational movement due to its unique formation. Our bodies vibrate all the time between different frequencies. Our organs, thoughts, emotions, and external influences will create different frequencies. Even every feeling will cause a vibration.

Water molecules also vibrate at different frequencies according to their vibrational and rotational modes. These modes have a quantum origin. Every hydrogen and oxygen atom in the water is subjected to energy vibration. This emits a distinct resonance. These resonances can be measurable by an electromagnetic frequency.

Under normal circumstances, water molecules synchronise into a single frequency. However, when this rhythm is disturbed, water undergoes a fascinating transformation. The frequency will change to waves of superimposed frequencies and due to this, water will achieve a superposition that breaks the molecule into its elemental constituents. Further, a free atom is recombined and forms diatomic molecules. H2 and O can play oddly with the resonances as the water molecule could act as a radiator and receiver of frequencies. That's why water is always with dancing molecules and not at the state of simple H_2O.

Recently, scientists have probed the quantum spectrum around the DNA of pure water. The revelation explained a DNA-like structure within water with an added dimension. This complex system radiates some waves which can move and produce conditions and situations to neighbouring water. This phenomenon is termed "DNA transduction". Many scientists believe that water memory is the result of this DNA transduction linked with resonance and frequencies.

This position made water, a mediator between the energetic and material world and functions as an accumulator, transmitter and transducer of energy patterns and information. When water is in contact with situations, it memorizes energy patterns and retains the energetic memory of vibrational frequencies for extended periods.

The study investigating water's DNA and its quantum interactions proposes that water can be aptly characterised as *"Living Water".*

The concept of Living water is very much in the fabric of all religions. Most religions believe that water has a life of its own. Even today, science shows us that a single drop of water is home to many tiny creatures, sometimes, as many as 36,000.

That's why getting truly pure water is nearly impossible and many experiments failed because of it.

In 2013, John Priscu and his team collected water from Lake Whillans in Antarctica. This lake is isolated from any human intervention for a million years and he wanted to find out if any life is present in such water. During the analysis, they found 130,000 cells in each millilitre of water with more than 4000 species of bacteria and other microorganisms.

Whenever scientists try to study water, they usually focus on the basic structure, the H_2O molecule. However, water molecules are never found alone. Water does not exist as a single molecule. They are always connected to others through hydrogen bonding or polar bonding, having bulk water properties and behave accordingly.

Scientists mainly study molecular processes through computer simulations. This approach is due to the current limitations in technology which prevent us from directly tracking a vast number of molecules. The methodology involves capturing snapshots of molecular activities within short timescales and monitoring various parameters such as environments, reactions, trajectories, and other relevant factors. These collected data are then input into supercomputers, which make the simulations of the molecular world.

Much like creating a complicated video game, these computers can calculate the path, fields of attraction, influence, repulsion, and other dynamics. The simulations can be made to reflect various situations, considering variations in temperature, pressure, density, volume, and so on. The accuracy and details of these simulations allow scientists to conduct a detailed analysis and behaviour pattern of bulk substances.

However, this simulation study will not help in the case of water. Making a computer model of water is extremely difficult as the way two water molecules approach each other is very complex.

A single ice crystal contains ten sextillion molecules, and all these molecules are rearranging themselves all the time. These constant rearrangements give a distinguished character and shape. No one has ever seen a water molecule and it does not exist in isolation.

Any attempts to draw comparisons with similar molecules from other substances will give only a false idea. Water is beyond the standard molecular perspectives and defies predictable analysis. Water is an abundant substance.

Due to advancements in science and quantum physics, we may be able to isolate water molecules in future. However, it might not give us an opportunity to do a comprehensive study and the answers we are looking for. The water molecules in a group (bulk water) behave differently from isolated molecules due to their unique characteristics and anomalies. The ancient idea of water being a living entity or living water gaining a reputation even today because of these fascinating qualities of water.

When we jump into the water from a height, a particular force will pull us upward. The pulling force is more prominent the deeper we go. The water around us transforms remarkably. Similarly, observe and check the water at the top of the waterfall and its state after the falls. Water from the top is normal but after cascading from a height, it takes on a sticky and elastic quality. As the water settles and starts moving, it gradually returns to normal.

Instances like ice floating, water defying gravity to reach tree heights, its expansion in lower temperatures or its role in the germination process, all are manifestations of structural changes. All these examples, explored in this book, showcase the unique behaviour of water. Water understands the situation and adapts its structures accordingly. Some kind of intelligence is involved in the water. Once the situation is managed, it returns to its original state. This awareness, a distinct phase in water's behaviour, attributes water as unique and powerful. This makes water *"conscious water "*.

The origin of water on earth remains a subject of investigation, with various theories explored in this book. While our understanding is continuously evolving, we can conclude one thing without any doubts. Water is an extraterrestrial substance. Water arrives on earth from somewhere or produced with the help of some external force. The enigma of water's origin is shrouded in mystery. We find ourselves unable to definitively ascertain its genesis. This significance underscores the "God given" status of water, a status of *"Divine water"* or *"Holy water"*.

The next profound significance of the water that we recognise is that water is produced due to some kind of combustion or similar process. Hydrogen and oxygen are easily available to us, but despite this availability, producing water in the lab is not an easy task. Mixing Hydrogen and oxygen does not produce water. Substantial energy is required for this transformation. The union and separation of hydrogen and oxygen involve significant energy interferences. Here it comes to another understanding from a different perspective.

Water possesses two energy sources - kinetic and potential. Water uses kinetic energy for movement and flow. Potential energy is stored and utilised when needed. Normally, molecular attraction generates certain potential energy, but water exhibits a very high level of potential energy.

The ocean waves and tides are significant examples of how the Sun and Moon exert their influence on water. The rise and fall of the tides over the sea is generally caused by the gravitational pull of the Moon. The gravitational pull creates a bulge in the ocean towards the side facing the moon, and the Earth's and Moon's rotation creates a centrifugal force on the Earth's surface. Based on this, high tides and low tides happen. This phenomenon is happening in the oceans twice a day.

However, it is not only the moon that is instigating this gravitational pull. The Sun too actively participates in the tidal forces relatively half the strength of the moon. These solar tides also repeat twice a day, and both individually act to establish the rhythm in the rise and fall of the tides.

The Sun and Moon power the energy to water and the water absorbs it. Many scientific studies concluded that the Sun is the primary source of energy. As per these studies, water absorbs light energy from sunlight. This energy is stored and subsequently utilised in various ways, such as powering our bodies, plants, and soil.

Plants use radiant energy to grow, and water uses it for movements. Many times, it transduces photonic energy in a manner similar to the plants. Like the Sun's energy, water also absorbs the energy from the Moon. There is an energetic connection between the elemental water, Sun, and Moon.

When water absorbs this radiant energy from the Sun, any information contained in the energy is also absorbed by water. Based on the structural variants, water may store or lose this information or sometimes it emits along with energy. We can feel the radiant energy when our hands circle a glass of water as it can feel and absorb this energy. Any information retained with water will lead to electromagnetically communicated structural formations. This kind of information can be transmitted as DNA-structural signals to water. Water's consciousness can be interpreted with this phenomenon.

A recent discovery by scientists at the University of Hawaii found that high-energy electrons originating from the Earth's plasma sheet are contributing to the formation of water on the moon's surface. Also, data from India's successful moon missions, Chandrayaan-1 and Chandrayaan-3, found that these electrons are breaking rocks and minerals on the lunar surfaces, potentially aiding the water formation process.

Many religions and cultures around the world align their festivities and rituals based on lunar and solar cycles with water, effectively indicating the connection between solar energy, lunar energy, and water. Even the controversial linking of the menstrual cycles of women to the moon is an interesting subject for scientific studies as the menstrual cycle length and Moon cycle length are almost similar. The consciousness of water's ability to store and utilise energy elevates the water to status, the status of *"Energy water".*

When you see a tribe or groups of people in the village, exhibiting similar behaviours, it might seem odd. It is a known fact that groups sharing a common water source tend to manifest similar kind of characteristics. They follow a collective conduct. Probably we call this concept "Sons of the soil". But soil has nothing to do with this behaviour. It is water that serves as the unifying factor.

I have dedicated some chapters to talk about various belief systems to shed light on the universal recognition of water's power. Despite our social divisions based on caste, creed, colour, religion, language, country, and ethnicity, water stands as a unifying force for us.

In ancient times, the strategic placement of temples, churches, mosques, and other places of worship near water sources reflected an understanding of water and spirituality. This deliberate proximity to water was not a coincidental act, but a way of recognising the transformative power of water and arranging to harness it through rituals.

For Muslims, the ritual use of water before prayer extends beyond physical purification. In Christian traditions, the act of Baptism goes beyond symbolism. Hindu practices involving water are not a gesture of gratitude. Beyond the symbolic gestures and religious narratives, water assumes a literal role in shaping our well-being and perspectives.

The water we drink courses through approximately 60,000 miles of arteries and veins, connecting every organ, and engaging with our physical, mental, and energy dimensions. Each sip of water is a transformative experience, offering a chance to elevate our bodily functions, mental compassion, and energy balance.

Modern medicine is based on molecular aspects of biological and pharmaceutical research. One of the basic and most challenging factors for clinical research is getting a new molecule. Worldwide, government bodies and pharmaceutical companies are spending billions of dollars every year on molecular clinical research. They succeed in lab trials most of the time, but success rates drop drastically in human trials. The underlying reason is that the human body is very complex and is never fully understood.

This is more accurate when we talk about the relationship between water and our sophisticated mechanism. A human-applied perspective is needed to understand the relationship. We have so much knowledge about water, but compiling and utilising this knowledge for our well-being is lagging behind. Once we have all areas of information in place, with proper understanding, we can potentially discover cures for various illnesses and enhance our well-being. This is the time to leverage our collective wisdom.

Chapter 8

Water – Ideas for Life (WIL): An Introduction

"Om Poornam Adah Poornam Idam
Poornaat Poornam Udachyate
Poornasya Poornam Aadaay
Poornam Evaa Vashishyate"

That (Brahman) is whole, this (creation) is also whole, from that whole (Brahman) this whole (creation) has come out. But even though this whole has come out of that whole, that whole remains whole only.

– Isha Upanishad

The creation and everything manifested from it are complete. Consider our body as a simple example - it consists of billions of cells - still, each cell is complete by itself. Millions of cells join to create our organs and body. When humans reproduce, that is also complete. Microcosm in macrocosm.

The same applies to every elemental thing. You can get the same properties in a small part of any element. However, this elemental theory does not apply to water. Two snow water crystals are not the same. Earth has billions of snowflakes stored for millions of years. But if you experiment with it, every flake is different.

This strange formation has similarities with our physical and mental structures. No two individuals are the same, similar to snowflakes. This individuality carries over to how we approach water in our daily lives. When to drink, how much to drink, and the various ways water can impact our overall well-being, differ from person to person. To maximise its benefits, understanding our water usage is essential. Let us embark on this exploration.

Our connection with water starts from the inception of foetal development. The journey starts across three stages in the womb - germinal, embryonic, and foetal. The germinal stage marks the initial phase of pregnancy through fertilization. Followed by the embryonic stage, where a fertilised egg implants the uterus lasting till about the eighth week of pregnancy. The foetal stage begins around the ninth week and continues until birth.

During these stages, our existence develops in water. The germinal stage necessitates water as a conduit for sperm transport. Sperm cells swim through the cervical mucus - primarily composed of water - to reach the fallopian tubes where fertilization takes place. The amniotic sac, which surrounds and protects the developing embryo, is filled with amniotic fluid.

We have already discussed the role of amniotic fluid. This connection with water continues throughout our lives. In our five senses, the first feeling we experience is "Water". By around the sixth week onwards during our womb stay, we develop all five senses through water. The food choices that mothers make during pregnancy can influence our preferences and tastes later in our lives. Similarly, studies suggest that a mother's emotional state during pregnancy can impact the baby's development and the foundation of emotional well-being. A recent study found that even a child's language preferences can be centred on what he is hearing from his mother's womb. Water is the bridge for transmitting all these experiences in our womb stay.

Every time we drink a glass of water, trillions of water molecules enter our bodies. Many similarities exist between water and us. The density of water is equal to the density of our body. The mineral composition in both water and our bodies has striking similarities. The mineral compositions of our cells are similar to the mineral composition of seawater. The frequency of the sound of water matches the frequency of our breath.

We are in a scientific & technological world. We have more comfort than any of our previous generations due to the vast technological advancements. However, we always have an isolated approach towards the life process. We want to understand life as a progression of events, a step-by-step process and not as a whole. Maybe due to this, we often don't consider water as a complete entity.

Over centuries, our methodical but narrow approach towards the environment created many problems with water. We have used it without fully understanding it, often going against natural law, and facing long-time consequences.

The health benefit of water is documented enough and has been practised over centuries. However, all practices are performed using clean and naturally purified water. Water pollution wasn't a concern in earlier times as our natural abundance was not disturbed. Water was enriched with purity and vitality.

Today, we are hesitant to drink untreated water due to widespread contamination. Groundwater, once clean, is now contaminated with pollutants, pesticides, and chemicals. Natural resources like rivers, ponds, wells, and lakes are no longer suitable for direct consumption due to high pollutant levels. As a result, we rely on treated water or commercially produced mineral water. Even in our homes and offices, water filters have become a standard. The question is: Is the treated water we consume good?

Accessing pure water become increasingly challenging in our times. Even though the water looks very clear to our eyes, it is loaded with many contaminants. Even rainwater falls victim to atmospheric pollution. Having understood the problems, we should explore remedial measures.

In our environment, most of us don't have the luxury of having pure water from mountain streams or an unpolluted aquifer. We must adapt to the available water sources. However, within this constraint, we can still make our lives better with water. Thankfully, numerous methods and ideas exist to enhance the characteristics of the water. These are the ideas for life.

Before delving into it, first, let us assess the quality of our water. A basic understanding of water treatment methods will help in finding the technical reliability of it.

Chapter 9

Water – Ideas for Life (WIL): How Pure Is My Water?

"The water in a vessel is sparkling; the water in the sea is dark. The small truth has words which are clear; the great truth has great silence".

– Rabindranath Tagore

When water descends from the sky, it is tasteless and odourless, representing its purest form. However, as it interacts with the sun, air, and moon during its descent, it gets a different kind of quality. Raindrops, dew, stormwater, and snow water have varied qualities and seasonal variations also can bring changes in these qualities.

In Ayurveda and Eastern traditional systems, water quality is categorised based on these variations and atmospheric conditions. As per Ayurveda, *Gangambu*, resembling Ganga gel, considered as purest form of water, while *Samudra* represents the most contaminated water. In between these extremes, seven different types of water are categorised based on their qualities and the sources.

Mountain runoff, water filtered through sand pits, water from streams or rivers, and well or pit water are deemed suitable for consumption. Similarly, water from certain rocky reservoirs with a sweet taste and clear appearance seems fit for therapeutic usage. Water sourced from trees, waterfalls, water gushing out from springs and lakes replenished with fresh water annually is also considered drinkable.

In my childhood, during pilgrimages with my grandfather and his friends, they always carried some cooked white rice with them to assess water quality. Along the journey, they collected water, placed the rice in it, and observed colour changes over a period. If the rice retains its white colour, they consider the water to be pure and drinkable. This method was commonly practised in many Indian villages in earlier times. However, the current reality is that most natural water resources are significantly contaminated, and we are forced to carry bottled water. This contamination prompted us to investigate the purity of water.

Let us first examine the urban or rural pressurized water supply system. Firstly, water is sourced from intake areas located away from our living spaces and transported through a high-pressure pumping system. It is a brutal way of water transport. The use of high pressure, occupied with narrow pipelines, numerous bends, twists and turns, along with violent motions, together change the water into a different form. By the time it reaches the reservoir, it is referred to as "dead water". The water cluster undergoes fragmentation during this journey, leading the way to losing its energy and characteristics.

Subsequently, in treatment plants, water undergoes an array of chemical and biological purification processes. Chemicals like coagulants and flocculants are added in a vigorous mixing condition to facilitate the removal of suspended, at times, dissolved solids. Chlorine or similar oxidant is added to act as a disinfectant for the removal of harmful microorganisms. A filtration process is employed to remove the fine suspended particles.

After this treatment process, the water continues its journey through the same forceful transportation system to reach our homes. Finally, when water arrives at our taps, its energy and life are lost in transit. We have sophisticated infrastructure to collect, treat, and deliver the water to our homes. However, the process compromises the essential qualities of water we use for drinking, cooking, and bathing.

Water chlorination is a widely adopted method for disinfecting. Chlorine is a powerful disinfectant and very effective in killing viruses, bacteria, and other microorganisms, thereby preventing water-borne diseases to a greater extent. This method is preferred due to availability and cost-effectiveness.

When chlorine is present in water, diseases are away. But when we consume chlorinated water, it can lead to toxicity, vomiting, and stomach issues. Hence, it is not suitable for drinking or bathing. Some of you may have experienced eye irritation and body itching while swimming in a pool disinfected with chlorine. Elevated chlorine ingestion can be extremely toxic and deadly to humans. The reaction between chlorine and minerals in water can produce Trihalomethanes (THMs), associated with health issues like asthma, cancer, and other heart issues. Chlorine gas has been historically used as a chemical weapon during war. Chlorine can surely eliminate microbes, but it can also be fatal for humans too. Unfortunately, monitoring the chlorine level in water is often neglected.

We can smell chlorine in water, but that does not mean there is no presence of it. It can stay in water at minute levels, and prolonged consumption can damage our vital organs. Devices such as activated carbon filters are available in the market for dechlorinating water.

Chlorine is unstable and tends to evaporate easily. Chlorine will react with water and form hypochlorous acid. Then it will dissociate itself and form hydrogen and hypochlorous ions. Further dissociation will leave the chlorine in gaseous form and release into the atmosphere. However, the reactions are based on the level of chlorine, temperature, and the pH of water. Boiling water is an effective home remedy to remove chlorine.

Earlier, packaged drinking water or bottled mineral water was a status symbol and indicated luxury. Nowadays, it has become a commonplace item and is consumed by everyone. Bottled water or packaged drinking water plants employ multiple stages of filtration and chemical treatment to ensure the water's quality. The perception of water quality has evolved and a higher level of purification results in better water.

The initial step involves chemical treatment and sand filtration to remove suspended matter. Subsequently, disinfection followed by fine particle removal is employed. Depending on the source, water further undergoes treatment in a pressurised membrane filtration process such as ultrafiltration and reverse osmosis. Before packaging, water is further treated with ozone or ultraviolet rays, or a combination of both, for additional disinfection. Whether it is treated tap water, packaged drinking water, or bottled water, the very condition of water remains the same. In today's scenario, the exhilarating taste and essential benefit of fresh drinking water are a dream for all of us.

Today, many of us already have a water purification device at home, and those who don't may acquire one soon. Our process of buying water purification devices is often influenced by advertisements, recommendations, and other factors rather than a clear understanding of what suits individual needs.

Like a doctor requiring a diagnosis to understand the illness, it is important to analyse the water to determine the suitable device. Let me give a glimpse of the physicochemical properties of the water which will make you a more informed consumer.

Water impurities can be broadly classified into physical, chemical, and biological contaminants. Physical impurities such as turbidity, colloidal and suspended particles can be removed using sizing filtration. Basic sediment filtration devices with a filtration range of 5 to 10 microns can remove these impurities and we can get visibly clear water. For an understanding, the size of a human hair is 40 to 60 microns.

Biological contamination is more dangerous than physio-chemical contamination. Identifying these contaminants is a problem as affordable and widely available methods are not available. The size of most harmful microorganisms and viruses is typically larger than 0.45 microns. Microorganisms can create lots of health issues, and some are even deadly. Waterborne diseases such as cholera, typhoid, dysentery, and hepatitis can be transmitted through biologically contaminated water. Filters with activated carbon, Ultrafiltration Filter (UF) or Ultraviolet (UV) technology can eliminate these microorganisms to a greater extent. If the water is from open sources like surface water or lake water, the above types of filtrations can give visibly clean and pathogen-free water. This way we can keep the minerals in the water intact.

Rainwater serves as a major source of pure water for us. However, it is subjected to atmospheric contamination. As water descends to the ground, it absorbs minerals as it moves through the earth. The water also absorbs carbon dioxide from the atmosphere and plants, giving it a slightly acidic nature. Once it comes into contact with earthly minerals like calcium and magnesium, it reacts and forms soluble bicarbonates. The nature of water changes from slightly acidic to slightly alkaline and water becomes hard.

Moreover, depending on the land it traverses and stores in, water can pick up minerals like sodium, chlorides, sulphates, nitrates, heavy metals, and other substances. The universal solvent nature of water makes it susceptible to contamination with any soluble substances. The volume of these dissolved substances can be higher in the summer seasons because water has stronger dissolving power when it is warm.

Reverse osmosis (RO) based filtration device is a popular choice today. RO is a molecular-level filtration process that can separate minerals and nutrients in the water. It can make hard water soft. Minerals are good and essential for the body. But excess minerals are not advisable. Excessive mineral intake can create health issues. RO filtration is a preferred choice when minerals exceed the drinking water limit expressed in milligrams per litre (PPM), or some minerals exceed the acceptable level.

As a general practice, total dissolved solids (TDS) between 50 to 300 ppm are considered good quality drinking water. Water having TDS between 300 to 500 ppm is considered poor quality but drinkable, whereas TDS exceeds 500 ppm is not suitable for drinking. RO also can tackle other contaminants like iron, fluorides, arsenic, pesticides, and microplastics.

However, RO water is often tasteless and acidic in nature. Commercial RO unit manufacturer sometimes infuses chemicals such as sodium carbonate, calcium carbonates, limestone, or proprietary chemicals to add taste and neutralise the acidic effect. But naturally occurring salts like rock salt, Epsom, and Bamboo salt are recommended for remineralisation to avoid health issues associated with artificial mineral infusions.

Choosing the right water purification device is important to maintain the physio-chemical balance of drinking water. Even though a comprehensive water analysis is preferred to understand the physio-chemical characteristics of water, a simple test of pH, total dissolved solids (TDS), total hardness (TH) and total suspended solids (TSS) will give a basic idea of the characteristics of water. These tests are very cost effective now and even readymade kits are available for home testing.

Seasonal variations can impact the water quality. Rainy season will increase suspended, biological, and turbid matter in water. Summers will increase minerals and dissolved solids in the water. Selection of water purification shall be done based on periodic water analysis considering the water sources and seasonal changes.

Normally, drinking water should slightly be alkaline with a pH of 7 to 8. The total hardness of the water should be less than 100 milligrams/litre as CaCO3, and suspended and biological impurities shall be nil. Special attention should be given to iron, lead, arsenic, fluoride, boron, mercury and chromium, as these can lead to severe health complications even at a minute level.

Heavy metals should be removed before drinking and the level of noble metals shall be as minimum as possible.

The purification device shall be tailored to the water quality which can ensure an appropriate level of treatment. Over-purification can result in more complications than benefits. A knowledge-based approach is beneficial for selecting purifiers based on water quality, source and seasonal changes.

Living in rural areas often gives access to natural water resources like ponds, wells, springs, and rivers. This water is more energized compared to tap water and can be directly consumed. Springwater, especially from the mountains, is the most suitable drinking water. However, pollution and our behavioural consequences, often render these waters unsuitable for direct use. In many parts of India, rural communities employ a simple yet effective method using traditional attire, like cotton sari or *mundu (veshti)*, for water purification.

This idea involves folding the *sari* or *mundu* eight times and passing the water through it, aiming to remove sediment and harmful bacteria. Through personal experiments, I have found this method to be remarkably successful, achieving over 90% removal efficiency for suspended matter and harmful bacteria. This idea is worthwhile when alternative sources are not available.

Whatever treatment method we adopt for purifying the water, it is important to note that purified water is not inherently pure. Beyond physio-chemical purifications, water requires attention and relaxation after treatment. Water needs to regain its cluster form to truly thrive. A pure state of water is difficult to obtain with our modern distribution and purification method. This raises important questions.

How to restore water in its pure form?

How to make live water from dead water?

How to vitalize the water?

We can explore some ways in the next chapter.

Chapter 10

Water – Ideas for Life: Energizing Water

---

*"On the last day, the great day of the feast,
Jesus stood and cried, saying, if any man thirst,
let him come unto me, and drink. He that believeth
on me, as the scripture hath said, out of his belly
shall flow rivers of living water".*

— John 7:37-38

Many use the term "dead water" for the pressurized water we drink. Let me simplify the explanation of dead water. When the water becomes stagnant for a long time or transported through violent conditions, the crystalline nature of water is broken, oxygen-depleted, and the vitality is lost. This condition is referred to as "dead water". This can be compared with the decay that occurs when blood circulation stops in the body.

There is a vast difference between stagnant water and moving water. Stagnant water or treated water from the tap lacks liveliness. Although water does not possess the qualities to grow and produce, it is intimately connected to the life, reproduction and growth of all living organisms. Water in a stagnant phase is considered dead water because it lacks the dynamic qualities expressed through movements.

When water is in motion, it oscillates between various shapes and forms. A river or stream will never flow in a straight line. It always follows a zigzag path. As the water meanders, it has a flow within the flow, a downward flow and a revolving flow across the stream's axis. This simultaneous dancing is due to the interaction of two forces - the natural tendency of water to form a spherical shape and the gravitational pull. In this dynamic state, the inner tendency of water is one of the reasons why it is referred to as "living water".

As we saw in the earlier chapters, when water flows through our bodies, it carries unique characteristics along with it. The state of the water will decide the quality of the occurrences in various ways. Dead water can be more harmful in the overall process. If the quality of energy in the water is weak and detrimental, it impacts our body and mind.

When water flows through our bodies, it takes an impartial route, merely carrying whatever it contains, influencing our body and mind based on what it contains.

More than the body, our brain and blood are particularly influenced by the water. The brain is composed of 80% water and the plasma in blood is made up of 90-92% water. Have you ever wondered when you are stressed or feeling weak, taking a shower makes you feel relaxed and calm?

Over the centuries, many methods have been developed to enhance the energy and vitality of water. I can give details of some of these proven and time-tested techniques.

In the revitalization process, the way water is stored will play a major role. Our forefathers used clay vessels and earthen pots for storing water. Most clays are slightly alkaline in nature which stabilizes the balance of water to a certain extent. The micro-texture block in the clay not only blocks some contaminants but also makes water breathe into this. It is the connection of water with its own nature.

The traditional water pots and vessels were crafted with a specific shape for centuries. These pots are made with egg or sphere-like shapes. In these shapes, the receptive potential of water is maximized. The energetic state and equilibrium can be achieved faster in these shapes due to the absence of stagnant areas. Depending on the climatic conditions outside, the water breathes and cools through the micro-texture blocks in the clay pot. The clay's porous structure and breathing forces cool water at the bottom while warmer water rises to the top. The pot design and the material enhance the circulation energy, maintaining a natural and continuous movement that aids in water revitalisation.

Eastern civilization provides a deeper understanding of the egg and sphere shapes. They believe keeping water in these shapes infuses it with a specific energy. The egg and sphere shapes embody masculine and feminine poles. The narrow end represents the masculine pole, and the wide end represents the feminine pole. Pot design is tailored based on this concept, influencing the energy dynamics of water stored. Depending on the placement of the narrow-end and wide-end in an upward motion, the water with masculine and feminine energy is available. *Yin* is masculine and *Yang* is feminine energy. Accordingly, *Yin* water is used for drinking and *Yang* water is used for plantation.

Similar to the wide usage of clay pots, copper vessels and bottles are highly regarded for water storage in India and various parts of the world. According to Ayurveda, storing water in copper vessels and consuming it can help balance the body's three doshas- *Vata, Pitta, and Kapha*. According to natural medical science, storing water in a copper vessel helps in its purification.

Copper can eliminate bacteria through a process known as oligodynamic effect. In simple terms, oligodynamics is the ability of some metals to exert and destroy the cells of bacteria. This antimicrobial effect is high in copper compared to other metals. When water is stored in a copper vessel, its ions slowly dissolve into the water. These ions can penetrate the protective outer membrane cells of microorganisms, disrupting the enzyme balance and effectively killing them. The traditional practice of keeping water in a copper vessel overnight and drinking it the next day is the simplest way to harness some health benefits. This includes balanced pH levels, relief from acidity, ulcers, and indigestion-related issues. Also, copper-infused water is considered an antioxidant, aiding in detoxification and stomach cleansing.

Beyond its antimicrobial properties, keeping water in copper containers has another aspect – resonance - the reverberating sound. Metals including copper resonate with emotions. Water also reverberates. Everything, living and non-living, has a vibrational frequency. Resonance occurs with all types of vibrations, connecting planets, stars, trees, animals, and humans. Even our emotions and thoughts have vibrational frequencies.

There is a connection between these vibrations and emotions, with some emotions having frequencies similar to some elements. The vibration of anger aligns with that of lead. Likewise, the vibration of stress is like that of zinc, and sadness aligns with the frequency of aluminium. Similarly, the vibration of steel and misery are similar. But copper vibrates harmoniously with water and gives it a revitalizing power. This may explain why our elders advised us not to store drinking water in aluminium or steel vessels, and instead recommended the use of copper containers for storage and consumption.

Another way of revitalizing the water is by introducing the vortex situation. Explosion and implosion are the two ways associated with energy. An explosion is a rapid expansion and release of volume and energy, as seen in a nuclear explosion or the functioning of an internal combustion engine. When our body and mind are in action, energy is released and consumed. When water is transported through a pressurized pipeline, it undergoes an energy release causing it to lose vitality.

Implosion is the opposite of explosion. It is squeezing. Implosion concentrates matter and energy. Applying implosion to water through vortex-like action can restore its energy and vitality. During the vortex process, an array of transformations will take place in water. It reactivates and restores its natural etheric energy. Water retains its natural health through spiralling, meandering, and winding motions. Nature takes care of these activities in many ways.

We can easily observe this phenomenon by stirring a glass of water vigorously. This action creates a vortex nature in water, demonstrating the implosion process. The continuous stirring not only dissolves more oxygen into water but also restructures it, making it more energetic and vital. Various devices are available in the market to facilitate vortex motion in the water. Keeping the water in pots after the vortex process can enhance the efficiency. The vortex process aligns with the natural motions of nature, which allows water to regain its etheric energy.

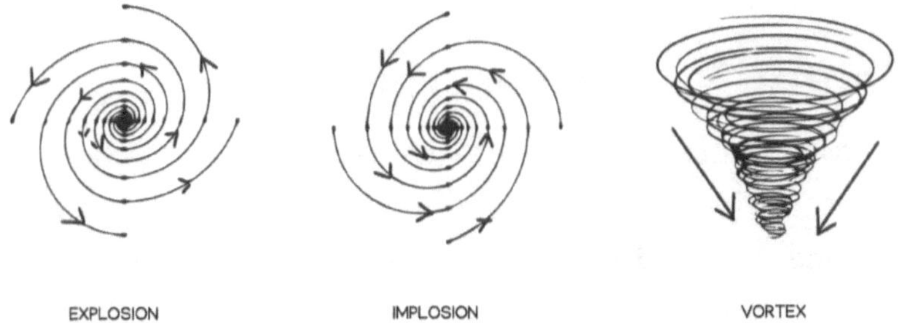

Fig 31 Vortex

Vortex energy is linked to the Marco systems of the cosmos. Leonardo da Vinci is one of the many personalities who studied vortex energy and made significant contributions to its applications and benefits. In the yogic sciences, *chakras* are often related to vortex energy.

Placing the water in the sun or exposing water to sun energy can be another method for water vitalisation. When sunlight permeates the water, it stores solar energy as potential energy. This potential energy is utilised by the water, converting it into kinetic energy, facilitating the restoration of its natural liveness.

Revitalizing and energizing the water is a process where a single method may not give proper results. Water subjected to drastic changes requires meticulous attention. The time frame for transformation is based on the circumstances and challenges the water faces. Revitalisation must be continuous rather than occasional. In addition to the process explained above, various techniques can be employed to further enhance the revitalisation and energising process.

Mantra, Yantra, and Tantra

Mantra, Yantra, and Tantra are systems or techniques practised widely in Eastern culture. Mantra means a process involving repeated chanting of sounds or words. Mantra is derived from two Sanskrit words *manas,* which translates to 'mind', and *tra* which means 'tool'. Mantra translates to "a tool for the mind".

Yantra means a pattern, object, or a machine. Tantra means a process, ritual, or work to expand. These three basic approaches are used for the constructive purpose of achieving peace, harmony, prosperity, and liberation. I am not presenting these techniques here from a religious or cultural perspective. It is used as a term to connect with water. In this idea, mantra stands for a formula, yantra stands for a device, and tantra for a process. You will understand this in the further readings.

The birth of the universe was initiated by a big bang, an outward explosion. Our universe ballooned outwards with matter in a fraction of a second. The latest investigation revealed that the sound generated during the Big Bang was humming. This humming continued for a long time till the universe grew large enough to fade the sounds away. The entire universe is in a state of vibration and every vibration produces a sound. Each vibration and sound has a unique frequency. In quantum physics, all substances are vibrations, whether it is an atom, electron, or nucleus, each having a different vibrational pattern. When we further explore the nucleus, it is nothing but a rotating wave.

The vibrational frequency of the human body is a fascinating aspect of our existence. From the microscopic level of cells to the broader systems, our bodies exhibit unique vibrational patterns. Vibrational frequency refers to the rate at which an object or system oscillates or vibrates. In the case of the human body, it involves the rhythmic motion of its constituent elements, such as cells, tissues, water, and organs.

Understanding and nurturing the optimal vibration frequency can contribute to overall health, vitality, and a sense of well-being.

The periodic table currently comprises 118 known elements. Out of this, 91 elements are naturally occurring, while the remaining 27 elements are artificially created via lab experiments. However, considering the traces of elements found naturally, the tally of natural elements goes up to 108. In short, native elements are 91 and natural elements are 108. Many scientists do not agree with the demarcation between native and natural elements. Elemental chemistry itself is a debated subject in the scientific community and remains an area for discussion and exploration.

Our human body itself is a testament to the elemental diversity present in nature. A human body is built with more than 90 elements. Similarly, animals, plants and other living and non-living things exhibit an elemental composition.

These elements along with the universe are constantly vibrating in a unique and separate frequency. Each frequency creates a unique reverberation. The whole universe and things in it are in a cosmic dance. When we align properly with this frequency, our life will align itself with universal consciousness.

In a common understanding, Mantras are a particular form of sound and a formula to align with a purpose. You can make and modify mantras with certain reverberations. Often, we wonder why many religious and spiritual chants have complicated and peculiar sounds and patterns. These are the product of comprehension of the relationship between sounds and their reverberations. These sonic formulas are designed to resonate with the fundamental frequencies of the universe, a conduit through which individuals can attune themselves to the cosmic rhythm.

In Eastern science, a human's life has multiple dimensions in it. The first dimension is pertained to the physical realm, where basic bodily functions take place. The second dimension is where our thoughts and material aspects unfold. The third dimension deals with the concept of energy or life force, called "*prana*". The fourth and fifth dimensions are based on consciousness.

Prana is life's energy mostly like *Qi* in Chinese and *Ki* in Japanese. It is in constant motion within our bodies in different ways. *Prana* also crosses through various active points in our bodies and these crossings are called *chakras*. *Chakras* are vibrating at unique frequencies. These reverberations of *chakras* have unique sounds.

Eastern traditions use these sounds extravagantly in wider ways, including prayer, healing, and daily activities. They intentionally create specific sounds based on certain conditions. These sounds are also known as Mantras. Mantras are practised or chanted with a specific rhythm. These mantras are widely used for energizing the water through recitation into water.

It is commonly believed that Sanskrit, one of the oldest languages, is derived from the vibrations of the *chakras*. Each Sanskrit letter represents a sound. This concept extends beyond Sanskrit. It extends to various ancient languages and the letters are formed with frequency or character attached to it. Chinese, Japanese, and Korean languages are based on characters rather than alphabets. Many Western, African, Latin and Native American languages also have unique relations with reverberation.

When we use the right kind of letters, words, or characters and pronounce them or chant them correctly, a particular reverberance will occur. This resonance, when we harness it in a specific way, can imbue water with energizing properties. You can form mantras in any language. Throughout civilisations, this method of energising water with sound and language was a common practice to rejuvenate water.

In temples, churches, or mosques, a system of music and chanting with rhythmic patterns is very common. They recite or sing in a particular way and use only selective instruments to do so. By doing this, a special type of reverberance occurs in these places which will help in the consecration of energy and aid the spiritual process.

Most classical music is closely connected to nature. They are inspired by natural phenomena and sounds. These music compositions have a structure and certain mathematics involved it. In Indian classical music, the *srutis* and *swaras* are made on inspiration and influence from nature. Similar in the case of Arabic, Western, and Eastern classical music.

Any classical music or sound from a classical instrument made with natural elements will produce a specific vibration each time.

When we observe religious, traditional, or civilizational customs, we see a distinctive practice, a rhythmic and repeated recitation of words or sounds. This repetitive custom can be found everywhere. When sounds or chanting are repeated multiple times in an exclusive place, a resonance field occurs in the surroundings. In theory, this is called the "morphic field".

When the sounds resonate, the place where the resonation takes place acts as a morphic field. We can call these places consecrated places or blueprint places of a particular reverberation. Churches, temples, mosques, monasteries etc., are examples of morphic fields. Water stored in these places is offered to people as holy water. These are energized water. Whether the sounds are good or bad, light or heavy, they will leave an impression on the water. These impressions will influence the water.

I have used the above details to give the essence and fundamental understanding of the power of sound and reverberation. We use the power of sound in many ways, unknowingly. How music and sound can affect us is a well-established scientific study. This harnessed power can be used for the energization of water.

Mantras can be anything, ranging from language to chants, words, phrases, music, and songs. Anything that collectively creates a positive ambience can be considered Mantras. If you are affiliated with any religion, use the chants and prayers relevant to your belief system. If you are a non-believer, use traditional instruments, light music or nice words. The factor does not lie in the medium, it lies in the reverberations.

Yantras are the conduits we use in this process. Simple devices like vessels, pots, and vortex devices are already discussed and can be considered as yantras. Tantra is the rejuvenation and repetition of the process which involves the above steps. In practical terms, this is what is meant by *Mantra, Tantra and Yantra*. When we use these ideas, we can energize the water and consuming it becomes a conduit for positive effects on our overall well-being.

Chapter 11

Water – Ideas for Life: Cautious & Conscious Drinker

"When life places stones in your path, be the water. A persistent drop of water will wear away even the hardest stone."

– Autumn Morning Star

Jan Baptist van Helmont was a prominent scholar born in 1580 and lived until 1664. He made significant contributions to the fields of chemistry, physiology, and medicine. One of his notable achievements was the theory of spontaneous generation.

The "willow tree experiment" Helmont conducted is considered the earliest quantitative study on plant nutrition and growth. He grew a willow tree for experimental purposes and measured the initial amount of soil, the weight of the tree, and the water he added. Over a span of five years, Helmont continued to monitor the tree's development and noted the changes in its weight and soil weight. The tree had gained 74 kg in weight over five years, but the amount and weight of soil were the same, with a loss of only 57 grams. Through a series of similar experiments, he concluded that the tree's weight gain and growth primarily derived from water. This experiment was a milestone in the history of biology.

The food we eat and the water we drink are the basis of our growth. The quality of food we consume and the water we drink can influence our overall health.

Doctors who practise various branches of medicine, all agree on one thing - the root causes of many degenerative diseases in the body are the results of prolonged dehydration. Being mindful of how we use water every day can make a big difference in our wellbeing. Just by making some conscious effort, we can help our bodies in many ways. Every function of our body is monitored and measured through the effectiveness of the flowing water.

For making this conscious effort, the first step is to pay attention to where the water comes from. An awareness of the surroundings of the water we consume. Many of us don't know the things that happen to the water before it reaches us. Hence, the first and foremost thing is to drink water cautiously and consciously.

Instead of drinking water directly from the tap or a flowing spout, it is better to use it from a device stored with water. Storing water in such devices will help the water to unwind and relax from its journey. Storing water in a copper vessel or clay pot is highly recommended. Water requires some time to unwind, and for this, 4–8-hour storage is a minimum requirement. Avoid storing the water in a plastic or aluminium container. Stainless steel containers can be used, but less preferable. The resonance properties detailed in this book can be the basis for selecting the materials for water usage.

Use plastic bottles only in unavoidable circumstances. If we are compelled to use plastic, make sure the material is PET (Polyethylene Terephthalate) and, drinking water standard is followed in the manufacturing process. However, PET is not suitable for multiple reuses and direct sunlight exposure. Most recent research by the National Academy of Science and Columbia University found that one litre of bottled water contains an average of 240,000 microplastic and nano plastic pieces. Micro and nano plastic accumulations in the body can create serious health issues. Also, it is estimated that about 1.3 billion water bottles are used daily, out of which, approximately, 60 million bottles enter landfills every day. It is better to avoid them for the sake of our health and environment.

Ensuring the vitality of water is a vital key to our well-being. The process of energization is a human physiology-based approach, which goes beyond just molecular aspects. Where we store water plays a major role in its energization. The good thing about water is its ability to transfer into different forms and return to its original state without losing its properties. No matter how much we abuse it, redemption is possible. Various methods for energizing water have been discussed before. We can adopt any of these practices.

The ideal place for keeping the water is important. It can attract and absorb certain energy, information, and reverberation. Hence, the surroundings should be clean and vibrant. The best place to keep the drinking water is not in our kitchen, it is in the prayer area. Most prayer places radiate positive vibrations. Prayers, regardless of our religious beliefs, are effective in creating positive moods. When water is exposed to this environment, it also undergoes a positive transformation.

Avoid placing water near the bathroom or electrical devices such as a TV, washing machine, or music system. We should avoid situations where water can expose itself to electrical energy and microorganisms secreting from bathrooms.

We can enhance the positive effect by placing a lamp or candle or incense near the water. Adding flower petals, herbs or leaves like Tulsi or Neem to the water is beneficial. Ayurveda suggests using certain flowers for water purification. If we put certain flowers in the water and leave it overnight, the water becomes drinkable. Utpala (Blue lotus), Naga, Champaka (Champak) and Patala (Rose flower) are the flowers commonly used. However, the efficiency and degree of purification with these methods are not well-documented so far.

When we pray, thank the water and express gratitude. You don't have to do this as part of any practice, do it just as a gesture of compensation for the harm we caused to water or an expression of gratitude for taking care of us. Water deserves that respect and recognition. It may look silly, but it works.

The next step is understanding how to drink water optimally. There are no specific rules on water intake in a day. It depends on the climatic conditions, intensity of activities, and our body conditions. Drinking excess water does not provide any added advantage. Instead, it can create a few troubles. Except on some occasions, small quantities of water in regular intervals are advisable, rather than waiting for a thirst signal. Too much water can drain the electrolytes from the body. But how much is too much? Let our body decide it.

As per Ayurveda, water is the manifestation of consciousness. Water is associated with lunar energy. Ayurvedic principles recommend a specific way of drinking water. It is advised to sit while drinking and avoid drinking while standing or lying.

Islam also promotes this concept. The prolonged habit of drinking while standing can disrupt the fluid balance and can lead to joint issues or similar complications over time. Drinking while sitting promotes muscle and nerve relaxation, aiding digestion and assisting the kidneys in the filtration process.

Starting our day with a glass of water on an empty stomach is an excellent practice. We should drink water before eating or drinking tea or coffee. Our kidney and stomach bladder will be happy to accommodate it. This approach is beneficial for cleansing our digestive system, removing toxins, and balancing stomach acidity. How much water to drink is a personal choice. But make sure you drink enough, maybe a stomach full.

Whenever you drink water, avoid gulping it down in one go. Instead, take measured sips, feel it, breathe slowly and appreciate each mouthful. If possible, pay attention to the sensation of water flowing through your body.

Optimal water consumption during meals is one of the most debated subjects today. Conflicting advice on whether to abstain from drinking during and after the meal or to drink during the meal is debated over and again. One of the best ways is to understand our physical nature and drink. It starts from our body structure and our digestion begins in the mouth with saliva and water. This aligns with the proverb, "Drink your food, chew your water".

For those coping with overweight or obesity, better to avoid drinking during the meal and immediately after a meal. Instead, having water at least 20 minutes before a meal allows saliva to naturally assist the digestion process. This can be more beneficial if the food is chewed properly while doing so. For those who have a medium build body, drinking water during the meal in small sips is beneficial. They can also have water before a meal but should have a minimum 20-minute gap after food. Individuals with lean and slim body physiques have more flexibility. They can have water as they wish. In short, the decision of water intake is guided by individual physical characteristics to a large extent.

Ayurveda describes a certain way people with *Vata*, *Pitta* and *Kapha doshas* should drink water with food. Individuals dominated with *Vata* dosha should drink water only one hour after the meal to digest the food properly. However, those with dominant *Pitta dosha* can sip a small amount of water throughout the meal to assist the digestion process. Similarly, Individuals with *Kapha dosha* should take water before a meal. Water balances the *Pitta dosha* supports *Kapha dosha* and counteracts *Vata dosha*.

Our emotional states, moods, and circumstances have an identical influence on water. When we are stressed or having mood swings, often we will get advised to drink water. When we are in a troubled situation, our inclination to seek solace in a glass of water is our intuitive response. The offering of water is a universal response to personal distress.

However, we must approach water consumption with awareness when we are in an agitated or stressed situation. Rather than drinking large amounts of water, it is beneficial to take it slowly and deliberately by calming our breath, syncing it, and sipping the water. This intentional approach will have a calming effect and will allow us to settle our minds gradually.

Being attuned to the environment when we drink is another aspect. Avoid consuming water in a noisy or crowded area and in unenviable circumstances like hospital ICUs, funerals, cremation sites, or accident sites. Our relationship with water is deeply personal and a private affair. And maintaining a sense of privacy in these situations is very essential.

When our body is going through vigorous activities like running, exercising, or fasting, consuming excessive water at once is not advisable, instead, adopt a measurable approach. Sipping water while sitting with intentional breath is the right approach to ensure hydration as well as harmonious balance.

When the water temperature is aligned with our body temperature, optimum results will be achieved. It is always good to drink water at room temperature wherever possible. While cold and warm water can offer specific health benefits under certain health conditions, extremes in temperature can be counterproductive. Still warm or cold water is preferable, it is essential to keep the temperature within a 4 to 6 degrees variation compared to the average body temperature of 37 degrees Celsius.

Many prefer, aerated or carbonated water in place of normal water. We commonly use the term 'still' for normal water and 'sparkling' for carbonated water. Still, water is good for proper and immediate hydration. Sometimes, sparkling water may be a choice for digestive or acid reflux problems as carbonisation may help to calm down stomach issues temporarily. But it is not a treatment. In the routine of consumption of water, it is recommended to drink it in its pure form. Sugary beverages, colas, and similar drinks are not the substitute for water.

It is important to follow some practices during bathing. When we bathe, our bodies absorb at least 1-2 litres of water. Regular bathing has many significant bodily advantages. This becomes more significant when we are stressed, tired or sleep-deprived, as bathing will help us to rejuvenate our body and mind.

An open bath in a river, stream, or a place where water is in motion is preferable, but it is a luxury today. Most of the time we use a pressurised water shower. It is convenient and easy, but pressurised water lacks the revitalising energy inherent in natural water resources.

Water kept in a vessel is good for bathing. It may not be possible to rely solely on vessel-stored water but consider storing water for some time and use it for final body washing. Indulging in a tub bath is more beneficial than taking a shower bath. We can elevate this experience by adding natural elements such as flower petals, naturally made aromatic oils and herbs. These additions not only enhance the sensory pleasure but also enhance the therapeutic and revitalisation effect.

In our older times, our forefathers employed a simple yet beneficial method to enhance the quality of water. They follow a practice that involves placing vessels filled with water under the sun for a period. As I mentioned in the previous chapter, it is one of the vitalization and disinfection techniques they followed for drinking and bathing. When sunlight falls on water, it enhances the molecular structure, imparting energy. Moreover, it makes water alive and energized. This water exhibits remarkable properties like being anti-viral, anti-fungal, and anti-bacterial. Water heated by sun rays and cooled by moonlight is said to be pure and has many therapeutic effects.

Scientific studies found that prolonged exposure to sunlight enables water to absorb vitamin D. The usage of this water helps our skin to glow and protects it from various allergies and rashes. Consuming this water will also help to cure digestive issues, heartburn, ulcers, and is also a great way to maintain bone health. It is recommended to allow water to bask in the sun for a minimum of 2 to 6 hours depending on climatic conditions before consuming or bathing. Best time to keep the water in sunlight is from sunrise to 3 pm.

The usage of warm water and cold water is another subject. Each offers a unique advantage on individual health considerations. For those having a healthy body, bathing in water having room temperature is most appropriate. During colder seasons, a refreshing bath in cold water can invigorate the body, and in hotter weather conditions, a warm water bath provides body comfort. However, we normally follow the opposite. We use hot water in winter and cold water during summer.

However, the best therapeutic approach involves using both cold and warm water in our bathing routine. Starting with warm water is the first stage of this therapeutic approach. This will help to expand the skin tissues and open skin pores. In this way, water penetrates easily into the skin.

Moderately, hot water will act as a stimulant. It improves blood circulation, pulse rate, respiration and makes the muscles more active. Following this, alternating between cold and warm water enhances the benefit. When we apply cold water after warm water, it will give a thermic impression to the body. The body responds to thermic impressions in several ways, benefiting us with an improved effect on blood circulation and a greater effect on the body.

This sequential switch, repeated 2 to 3 times, contributes to many physical and psychological benefits and overall skin health. The final rinse with cold water concludes the bathing. Maintaining equal duration for each warm and cold water cycle and avoiding harsh soap or gels during the bath will help to preserve the skin balance.

The majority of Japanese people follow a ritual called *"ofuro"*, a hot water bath before going to sleep. They believe *ofuro* can reduce fatigue, relax muscles, improve metabolism, promote good sleep and help them to relax after a hectic work schedule. They also have *Sento*, a traditional Japanese communal bath house all over the country for this purpose.

Humans are social creatures. We cruise through the twists and turns of life in the company of others. Most of our working hours are clocked in office cubicles, dedicating an average of 8 hours a day to our professional pursuits while consuming 1 to 2 litres of water throughout. Have we ever considered the significance of our water intake in our daily work routine?

The working atmosphere is not a leisure experience. Whether we are hustling in sales, marketing, managing projects or juggling with numbers, we all face our fair share of tasks and emotional rollercoasters. In the middle of these engagements, we often forget to keep ourselves hydrated.

Our brains will be busier with official engagements. We drink water only when we get symptoms of dehydration.

The repercussions of dehydration on our concentration and attention are already discussed in this book. When dehydration starts, it negatively impacts our physical and intellectual functions. This affects our professional competency. We can have a series of advanced physiological problems which are associated with dehydration and stress.

The physiological problems due to dehydration and stress are the same. Dehydration begets stress and stress will exacerbate dehydration. When our body detects dehydration and stress, a complex hormonal response is triggered. Our body initiates a fighting mechanism, leading to the secretion of several hormones persisting until the body gets out of stress. This is a threat to us in every way.

Water can be considered a potent ally in managing stress. By adopting some small changes and attentiveness, we can actively employ water as a resource in our arsenal against workplace stress.

The basic etiquette explained in this chapter is widely applicable when we drink water anywhere, whether at home or in the office. If we pay small attention to handling water in our working and social atmosphere, it will significantly benefit us in the long run.

In the office, we mostly drink water while standing due to the distance of the water dispenser or inadequate water in bottles. However, sitting and drinking is a better practice.

Smaller sips with deep breaths in between can promote good hydration and a moment of relaxation.

Prolonged sitting in our workstations can negatively impact our health. Health professionals recommend standing up every 20 minutes to avoid complications of prolonged sittings. They also suggest mild exercises for the eyes, legs, and hands. Use this time to have small sips of water, regardless of thirst. Let this 20-minute advice apply to water too. When we use water at regular intervals, we become more active, alert, and our productivity increases.

In many meetings and conferences, we spend a considerable amount of time, ranging from short to lengthy sessions. It is quite normal to sip water during these gatherings. However, have you ever considered the emotional atmosphere in the meeting room? The vibes and emotions present in the room can significantly impact water. Water does not recognize good or bad emotions. It does not distinguish between appreciation and anger. So, drink water only when the atmosphere is filled with happy feelings or positive emotions. If not, step outside the meeting room for a drink. Also, refrain from carrying water from the meeting room where heated arguments and uncomfortable situations occur. These meetings do not evoke positive emotions.

Long meeting sessions without a break are widely practised these days. People think a break in between will hinder their focus. However, our attention span is very limited. We can absorb only 20% of what we hear in 20 minutes. When we push ourselves to grasp more information, our brain tends to do the opposite. The more we try, the less our brain absorbs. Some studies suggest that humans forget 50% of new information within an hour, 70% within 24 hours and 90% within a week. Taking a water break every 20 minutes is more beneficial. It not only keeps you hydrated but also enhances focus and alertness.

An individual who performs multitasking often receives more attention and recognition in our office. Multitasking is widely considered a special ability. However, many studies found that people with high multitasking ability tend to suffer from reduced attention span and weakened memory. Also, their efficiency in switching between tasks is found to be quite low. Water is the best solution to mitigate these challenges. It plays a major role in preserving our attention, preventing distractions, and the development of specific neural networks in the brain.

Mild dehydration during working hours can affect our brain structures responsible for attention, thought processes, memory, and perception. These cognitive abilities are the basis of our performance and ability to fulfil responsibilities. However, many of us work in a dehydrated condition. When we are adequately hydrated with frequent water intake, the benefit is tremendous. It can enhance our visual memory, processing speed, reasoning ability, rational thinking, verbal recall and reaction time. It also improves the emotional and psychological states.

Place the drinking water in an area with as minimal human intervention as possible, preferably close to where sunlight is available. During moments of stress, or exhaustion, using cold water for washing the face and wiping the forehead with cold water proves effective.

When we focus on a task, it requires concentrated attention and consumes a lot of energy. Prolonged engagement can lead to a decrease in mental effectiveness and focus. In such a situation, it is better to shift your attention to a lighter or insignificant task and engage with them. This can provide the brain with an opportunity to relax and recharge.

Watching fish swimming in a tank has several positive effects on stress reduction and mood promotion. Many corporate offices have incorporated this concept for their employee's well-being. Biophilic design with water will be discussed in the following chapters. The gentle movements and soothing sounds of water can induce a relaxation response, reducing feelings of stress and anxiety. The repetitive and rhythmic nature of fish swimming can be meditative, promoting a sense of tranquillity and peace. Observing an aquarium can provide a welcome distraction from our worries and rumination. Since water has been associated with feelings of calmness and relaxation, it can redirect attention away from our stressful thoughts and help us to focus on the present moment.

Chapter 12

Water – Ideas for Life: Healthy Drinker

"Pure water is the world's first and foremost medicine."

— *Slovakian Proverb*

Water performs critical roles in our bodies, serving as a versatile substance with multifaceted responsibilities. As we have seen in earlier chapters, it acts as a solvent, building material, shock absorber, cooler, reaction medium, carrier of nutrients and wastes, lubricant, thermoregulator and many other significant bodily functions. However, its significance beyond hydration is poorly understood, and sometimes, wrongly manipulated. The secrets of water and its impact on health should have been the subject of extensive research.

Medicinal water or medicated water is a term that has gained popularity nowadays as a novel approach where water is used as a therapeutic agent. This involves the direct use of water as a medical substance or its supplementary use along with other medications to manage many health issues. Water has many secrets related to our health and wellness.

Numerous studies now underline water's curative and preventive potential in treating a wide range of illnesses like blood pressure, diabetes, migraine, arthritis, back pain, angina, asthma, cholesterol, Alzheimer's disease, ulcers, heartburn etc. More discussions regarding our health with water may lead to various hydrotherapy and medical processes. It is essential to approach this subject with a personalized and comprehensive perspective. Hence, the intricacies of medical processes are beyond the scope of this book. Readers are advised to consult healthcare professionals for appropriate therapy based on individual needs and conditions. Any general information can lead to misunderstanding or misinterpretation. Recognising this, I am limiting this section to some aspects of healthy water rather than health and water.

We spend between 30 to 60 minutes a day for external cleansing and grooming our bodies. However, amidst our focus on outward cleanliness, we often overlook the importance of internal purification. Terms like "detoxification" and "internal cleansing" frequently cross our paths. But we tend to ignore them until we are in some sort of health trouble. Water is not only used for an external wash but also an important medium for internal cleanliness.

Some scientists propose that, apart from its elemental chemistry, water has the potential to transform into organic matter. This hypothesis is derived from the observation of herbivorous animals developing kidney stones. Normally, kidney stones are composed of crystal-forming substances rarely found in grass and vegetables. This has led to the notion that stones are an act of "disguised water".

Consider the colon as our body's sewage system. On a day-to-day basis, we try to experiment with various types of foods and supplements. In India, over 50% of family outing time is devoted to exploring different kinds of foods and culinary delights. Additionally, we are constantly exposed to supplements, medicines, antibiotics, drinks, processed foods, and oily items.

Many times, the foods we consume and the medicine we ingest can exert adverse effects on our digestive system. Over time, the toxins, undigested foods, and chemicals will accumulate in our digestive tract. Initially, we may feel some inconveniences like stomach uneasiness, diarrhoea, constipation, and acidity which we solve with some home remedies or quick fixes. However, if it is left that way, these issues will escalate into severe health issues.

Colon hydrotherapy is widely used for cleaning our digestive system to remove the toxins and other accumulations that take place in our body over a period. This is a protocol-based therapy for our gut health which needs to be done with an experienced therapist. However, when we take lukewarm water on an empty stomach is one way to make our digestive system clean and healthy. This is the fastest way to get rid of waste from our bodies and repeated intake will improve our gut health.

According to the common theory of scientists, water has a special connection with cosmic energy. It acts like a cosmic sponge, soaking up this energy, and carries it wherever it flows. Moreover, water is always open to receiving more energy, and any changes in the overall energy makeup in the universe can affect the water.

Many wild animals can recognize this effect, which is why they select their water source carefully for drinking. We can use certain methods to infuse more energy into the water. Similarly, we can use certain methods to influence the water characteristics. Scientists have demonstrated an array of technologies to consciously prepare upgraded water. These methods can give an amplified benefit when we drink. They have come up with different methods like structured water, energized water, programmable water, alkaline water and hydrogen and oxygen-rich water.

Natural environments such as waterfalls or seashores, continuously release hydrogen ions into the air. Breathing this air can evoke a sense of well-being and energy. Hydrogen-enriched water is based on the theory of 'hydrogen depletion'. Hydrogen is recognised for its healing and antioxidant properties. It has a unique ability to reach every organ and cell in the body when we consume water. It neutralizes the toxic substances in the body and cleanses it. Hydrogen water is made based on the theory that hydrogen is the "fire of life" and not oxygen. Hydrogen is the fuel, oxygen is the fire, and water consists of both elements.

According to this theory, various organs store hydrogen, with the liver containing the highest concentration. The liver utilizes hydrogen to neutralize the free radicals during the detoxification process. Also, hydrogen provides protective benefits to the brain, particularly against strokes. This theory suggests that our modern lifestyles, dietary choices, and stress often lead to hydrogen depletion. Hydrogen-ionized water is a remedy for managing hydrogen depletion.

Scientists have developed many techniques to infuse hydrogen ions into the water. One simple method involves raising the vibration of water. Hydrogen attracts higher vibrations. Once the vibration is increased, it starts attracting hydrogen ions from the air. One scientist famously said, "Dancing water will have an affair with hydrogen ions".

Another method is to place a device in water that releases the hydrogen ion. Many devices are available for both methods, contributing to the popularity of hydrogen ion water. Recent studies suggest that hydrogen–rich water can play a role in reducing symptoms associated with diabetes and liver diseases.

The alkalization or pH adjustment is a concept centred around harmonising water with the body's natural chemistry. Some researchers indicate that consuming pH-balanced water can enhance the overall functioning of the body and mind. The human body tends to be slightly alkaline, with a pH range between 7.35 to 7.45, constituting majorly, blood pH. Naturally occurring waterfalls within a slightly alkaline pH range of 7.2 to 8.0.

However, the pH of water can be influenced by various factors such as storage conditions, type of water and treatment methods. Water's pH is influenced by the solids dissolved in it. Water which maintains the right pH balance possesses the ability to easily penetrate cell membranes, facilitating improved metabolic processes. This effective pH level also contributes to effective hydration. Alkaline water is for aligning the pH of water with the body's natural pH.

Magnetic water refers to the condition of water by passing it through a magnetic tube or by introducing a special magnet into the water. This process induces para-magnetism in the water due to its dipole moment. Scientists and doctors who are practising this technique claim that, when water exhibits para-magnetism, it transforms, becoming very fertile, and active. This results in a high oxygen ratio, and increased velocity of dissolved solids, and amino acids. Water transformed from its dead state to a more vibrant, lively state.

When water is exposed to a magnetic field, considerable changes occur in the pH, dissolved solids, hardness, oxygen, and bacterial count. Magnetic water acquires a finer and more homogenous structure which increases the fluidity, and the ability to dissolve various nutrients. Consequently, biological activities are improved. The surface tension of water is reduced by 10 to 12% and its velocity is increased compared to normal water. This facilitates easier penetration into cell walls, accelerating the diffusion of water, which can benefit different organs.

Individuals with kidney and gallbladder stone problems are often advised to consume magnetic water regularly. This process is believed to break down stones into tiny pieces, which can easily pass through urine. Many studies suggest regular consumption of magnetic water can aid in managing digestive, urinary and nervous problems, alleviate arthritis pain, reduce cholesterol deposit in veins and arteries, help to regulate menstrual cycles, and lower blood pressure. Nowadays, many experiments are being conducted to explore the use of magnetic water in animals for various conditions and in agriculture to increase crop yields.

Water functions according to the laws of nature. The vortex technology mentioned in this book is often used by many scientists to reenergize and revitalize water. In a natural environment, water flows in a cyclical pattern, like a vortex. This flow enables water to form a distinguished shape, mostly hexagonal. Rivers and streams exemplify this continuous dynamic flow with a distinct character.

However, when water is extracted, stored and transported, its equilibrium is disturbed, compromising its inherent properties. But when you mimic the water flow of nature in a device, we can reclaim its power and vitality. Across various parts of the world, vortex-based devices are employed to restore water to its pristine, natural state.

The recent popularity of water and its health-related benefits has unfortunately paved the way to organised scams exploiting people's curiosity and unfamiliarity. They make baseless health claims manipulate scientific terminology, fake testimonials, fake certifications, miracle cure claims, no-risk claims and fear tactics to promote their devices or technologies. In my opinion and personal experience, pure water is the best form of medicine when consumed appropriately. It can be used in our daily routine as a preventive and effective measure for promoting overall health and well-being. Focus on devices only when certain health situations arise and make an informed decision about buying such tools or devices.

Chapter 13

Water – Ideas for Life: Meditation & Water

"The mind is like water. When it is turbulent, it is difficult to see. When it is calm, everything becomes clear"

— Gautama Buddha

In my childhood and growing years, I had a humorous view of meditation. Whenever our school conducted any yoga or meditation sessions, we mocked it. I failed to appreciate how practices like maintaining silence, focusing on an object, or engaging in systematic breathing exercises could have benefits. My Western-influenced, proof-seeking mind never understood it rightly.

However, in recent years, there has been a remarkable shift in this perception. Looking back, I regret not recognising the value of meditation in my childhood.

Eastern culture has a rich history of widely embracing and practising meditation for thousands of years. This ancient science originated in the Indian subcontinent and became an integral part of Yoga.

In the early stages, meditation found its initial routes in Hinduism, Buddhism and Jainism, extending its influence across various parts of Asia. The philosophers of Taoism and Confucianism absorbed the essence of meditation, and it traversed across the Asian continent. Later it further spread in Western culture through the silk route.

The name meditation means "to ponder". However, meditation has more meaning in Eastern cultures. In Sanskrit, meditation is known as *Dhyana* which has a more profound and wider meaning than meditation used in English. I use *dhyana* here as a process of liberating mind from all disturbing and distracting emotions and as a flow of attention on a concentrated subject.

Prana, often described as the "Life force" is the energy dimension that sustains our existence. When a sperm and ovum come together, they form a cell called a zygote. This tiny cell eventually develops into a human body comprising over 10 trillion cells. Each cell interacts with each other and outside the cell with a tremendous complexity generated in one cell. Prana is driving that projection of awareness into our physical world.

We are alive because this life force is circulating inside us, keeping the body and mind together. Prana is more subtle than physical reality and less subtle than the mind. It is an intermediatory force between the body and mind.

We are getting certain *prana* from the environment by the act of breathing and eating. As we breathe, *prana* enters our lungs, and during eating, it is absorbed by the large intestine. Oxygen is the vehicle for our *prana* and is associated together. The lungs and large intestine are also associated with each other in the process of assimilating *prana* from the environment.

Water is the basic source of *Prana* when it is alive. Any natural water sources like streams, sea, and flowing water contain a significant amount of life force, often referred to as *Prana Jal*. Similarly, the air we breathe is often referred to as *Prana Vayu*.

The quality of *Prana* we take is influenced by the food, water, and living environment. The sustenance of the life process hinges on *prana*. Proper circulation and usage of prana promote a harmonious balance. When this circulation and usage is not proper, it can lead to problems associated with life energies.

It is important to use *prana* effectively for maintaining an overall balance in our physical, mental and energy realms. Unfortunately, no medicines have been specifically designed for managing this situation. *Dhyana* stands out as a fundamental method for purifying and enhancing *Prana*. Through meditation, we can facilitate the circulation of good *prana* while addressing and repairing any imbalances in the life force circulating within us.

Yoga, known as *Chitta vriti nirodhah*, aims to unite body, mind and soul and it is the way of life. When it is practised regularly, it gives tremendous results. The eight steps of yoga are: *Yama* (ethical guidelines), *niyama* (self-discipline), *asana* (physical postures), *pranayama* (breath control), *pratyahara* (withdrawal of senses), *dhyana* (meditation), and *dharana* (concentration), provide a comprehensive framework.

Within these steps, *dhyana*, or meditation not just a breathing exercise or relaxation technique. A broader understanding is required to comprehend the essence of mediation. Every person is unique in nature and meditation is to be understood based on this unique perspective. A wide variety of meditation techniques are developed worldwide to cater to the diverse needs of individuals.

In yogic science, the life force within our bodies is mapped out in a particular way. There are five kinds of life forces in us: *Prana* in the heart, *Udana* in the throat, *Samana* in the stomach, *Apana* in the trunk of the body, and *Vyana* pervading the entire body. These five *pranas* circulate through the body following a particular pathway called *nadis*, consisting of three main *nadis* and 72,000 sub-*nadis*. The primary *nadis*, *Ila*, *Pingala* and *Sushumna*, rise along the spine, with *Sushumna* extending from the base to the crown of the head.

As these *nadis* are intercepted, they form energy centres known as *chakras*. There are a total of 114 *chakras* with 108 considered active. Seven major *charkas* are aligned along with the *Sushumna Nadi*. *Chakras* are described as wheels but are usually symbolised by lotus flowers, representing purity in impurity. The *Muladhara chakra*, or the base chakra, is located at the base of the spine, followed by *Swadhistana*, or the *sacral chakra*, which is at the sacrum, *Manipura*, or nabhi *chakra* just below the navel, *Anahata*, or the *heart chakra* at the centre of the chest, *Vishudha chakra*, at the throat, *Ajna chakra* between the centre of the eyebrows and the *Sahasrara chakra* at the crown of the head.

Chakras and *Nadis* are from different perspectives and have different roles in the body. Their location is illustrative rather than precise. Basic knowledge is required to understand each perspective of *chakras* and *nadis.* You can find enough details from other sources as the scope of this book is limited to meditation and water. These seven chakras serve as the focal point of meditation.

The seven *chakras*, vital energy centres of the body, play a significant role in various aspects of meditation. Among them, the lower five chakras are linked to the five fundamental elements.

Mooladhara chakra, represents the earth, resonating with the sound "Lum" and is symbolised by a red-four petal lotus. *Swadhistana chakra* represents water, echoed by the sound "Vum" and symbolised by a six-petaled orange–vermilion lotus with a crescent moon. The six-petaled lotus symbols have a very significant meaning in Eastern culture. It is like the sixfold symmetry of snowflakes and found to have an affinity between the water and the number six. When water congeals into flowers, it naturally takes on a six-pointed pattern. This fantastic shape not only represents symbolism but also an actual form that can be observed through microscopic analysis.

Manipura chakra which represents fire, features a red triangle within a ten-petaled lotus, resonating with the sound "Ram". *Anahata chakra* aligns with air, symbolised by a green colour and the sound "Vum". *Visudha chakra* represents space adorned by a 16-petaled transparent white lotus resonating with the sound "Hum".

The other two chakras are not the representation of any elements and hence do not have a particular sound associated with them. However, the *Ajna chakra* is often associated with the sound *"Aum"*. *"Aum"* is not represented here as a religious symbol, but signifies the vibrational essence of the universe, a frequency of energy that connects all aspects of existence. The final two chakras, beyond elemental representation, serve as gateways to the higher consciousness.

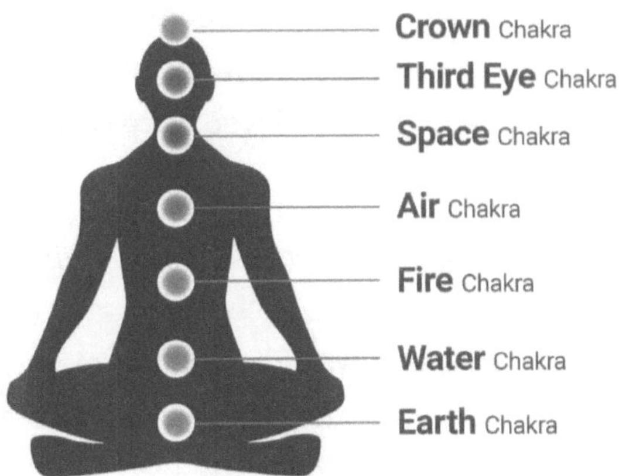

Fig-32 Chakras

In the yogic practice of meditation, *Bhuta suddhi* plays an important role in purifying and cleansing the five great elements that constitute the human body. Human body is made of five elements, of which four elements are actively participating, and the space element is considered a catalytic force. The human body, depending on the age, consists of approximately 65 to 80% water, 10 to 12% earth elements, 5 to 7% air, 3 to 4% fire and an empty space of 5 to 6% known as space.

These five elements are considered the basic building blocks of the universe, and all living things are composed of various combinations of these five elements. Through the practice of *Bhuta suddhi,* individuals engage in a meditative process focused on these elements, acknowledging their active participation in the body's composition.

The sounds associated with each element in *Bhuta suddhi* are designated for specific purposes in meditation. These sounds are crafted to elicit specific responses from body, mind, and energy. By integrating these sounds into the meditation process, a vibrational shield is believed to be created, fostering healing power.

Each sound can be considered a *beeja mantra,* or seed mantra, corresponds to a specific *chakra* and is intricately connected to the energy flow of associated elements. When recited in a particular manner, these sounds are believed to cleanse and activate the chakras, leading to an overall energisation of the entire body.

One can transform the well-being of the body and mind by doing the *Bhuta suddhi*, where the five elements of nature are under a certain control. *Bhuta suddhi* is often coupled with Pranayama (breath control) and dhyana (meditation). This combination proved to be more effective in harmonising and balancing the body and mind.

We can do the meditation focusing on all five elements or with specific elements. *Bhuta suddhi* is a very well-known practice of Hatha yoga. In meditation, there's no need to focus too much on materiality. Rather than focusing on the material aspects, the focus lies on experiencing the subtle sensation coursing through our bodies. The key is to immerse yourself in the feeling of water or other elements, allowing it to penetrate your awareness.

The *pranayama*, a breathing technique is the simple practice of this meditation. Focusing on the pulse and rhythm of the breath with the resonance utterance of the syllables is the common pranayama method for *Bhuta suddhi* meditation. The breathing can be belly breathing (diaphragmatic), abdominal or even breathing as per our convenience and choice.

The trinity of breath, visualisation and mantra form the connection with water in a meditative way. A combination of rhythmic control by breathing, the imagination of water flowing throughout our body and the sound *Vum* recited harmoniously surely give a meditative connection between us and water. This is the case with other elements too. However, it is advisable to learn *Bhuta Suddhi* meditation from an expert to maximise the benefits and avoid mistakes.

This connection through *Bhuta Suddhi* has a calming effect on the mind and nervous system. Water controls and governs the energy, fluids, nourishment, and purification of our bodies. By aligning with water through mediation, our mind finds peace, our emotions settle down and water brings tranquillity to our inner world.

Surya namaskar or Sun salutation is a widespread practice in yoga which involves 12 different postures or yoga asanas. This routine is designed to offer a range of physical and mental benefits in our daily lives. *Surya namaskar* not only benefits our physical body but also plays an active role in activating the chakras and aligning with the five elemental constitutions.

When we follow the 12 steps of Surya Namaskar, our body experiences the pressure and stretching which facilitates the activation of the chakras and smooth flow of prana throughout the body. *Surya namaskar* followed by *pranayama* and *Bhuta Suddhi* meditation is often referred to as a powerful tool for balancing energy and maintaining harmony between all systems of the human body.

Being with water itself is a form of meditation. Many such practices are available today for us and Ai Chi is one such system. *Tai Chi* is one of the popular life approaches that originated about 4000 years ago. It is a holistic approach that focuses on the flow of energy, known as "qi", reflecting and deciding the balance of body, mind, and spirit. *Tai Chi* practices are a combination of breath, movement, and meditation. It is a healing process often described as "meditation in motion". Drawing inspiration from **Confucianism and Taoism**, Tai *chi* aims to balance the *yin*, the masculine, and *yang*, the feminine energy, unblocking and encouraging the flow of *qi* energy throughout the body.

Ai Chi is part of *Tai Chi* and is a water technique. *Ai Chi* is an exercise-based holistic program for relaxation and rehabilitation of body, mind and spirit. *Ai Chi* is performed in a warm water environment thereby increasing the blood flow and maintaining the body temperature. This practice involves rhythmic and repeated sequences of movement of arms, legs, and torso with breathing techniques. Music and systematic procedure are often added to this practice.

Takigyo is a waterfall meditation practised in Japan. It is an ascetic meditation done while standing underneath a waterfall and letting the water pound us.

Zen meditation is based on Buddhist principles and is the pathway for achieving certain mastery over our mind. The goal of Zen meditation is to attain the state of "No Mind". This practice adopts many techniques involving water to amplify the benefits. Many times, flowing streams are used as an auditory tool in this meditation process.

Taoism, a culture based on water, often uses mental imagery of water for meditation. Floating in water, feeling the coolness of a river and concentrating on the body of water are a few processes used in Taoism meditation.

At any social gathering in Hindu, Christian, Jewish, Buddhist, and Muslim communities, there is a shared practice of spraying sacred water on the food before serving. In many civilizations, people used to engage in meditation before consuming food or water.

Since water meditation is gaining widespread recognition today, many parts of the world have curated specific types of meditation with water. Meditation in water is a straightforward process. It involves only expressing gratitude and respect. For those with religious affiliations, incorporating prayers while meditating can deepen the connection. For those who are without any religious belief, a simple expression of gratitude will suffice.

All and any forms are acceptable to water because, as the *Rig Veda* says, *"Ekam sat, vipra bahudha vadanti"* (Truth is one, sages call it by various names).

Chapter 14

Water – Ideas for Life: Being Water

"Empty your mind, be formless.
Shapeless, like water."

— Bruce Lee

An old man's principle for healing every situation is to drink a glass of water. Often, we see many situations, where people advise us to drink water. If we have headaches, are under stress, are scared, have sleep disorders, feel feverish, have cramps, exhaustion, or many other kinds of situations, the answer is usually, "drink water".

Water circulates 34 cycles in a year on Earth, and all these circulations happen without us even noticing about it. These circulations may appear the same, but a complex dynamism is happening within each circulation. Since ancient civilizations, water from mountains has been considered to have remarkable power and healing efficiency. The water from the high mountains, deep wellsprings, and forests is highly enriched and energized. One reason for this could be due to the water's less exposure to sun rays. Interestingly, water which is exposed to sunlight has certain benefits, while the one less exposed to sun has certain other benefits.

Being with Water

The crashing of waves, the flow of the river, or an impressive waterfall, the sights and sounds of water have a great impact on our well-being. There is a natural peacefulness in water that allows us to find solace and rejuvenation in its presence.

Waterfalls and seashores are the sources of negative and hydrogen ions. Have you ever noticed the water droplets rising upward from a waterfall? These droplets contain numerous charged particles abundant in these environments. We can call them "dancing ions". These ions are linked to various health and mental benefits including improved mood and increased relaxation. It increases the flow of oxygen to the brain and promotes serotonin production. Serotonin plays several influencing roles including happiness, memory, sleep, affection, sexual behaviour and so on.

The act of immersing oneself in a natural body of water has an impact on our mental and physical well-being. This connection with water allows us to experience a sense of weightlessness, enabling both our body and mind to find a state of relaxation. When we are submerged in water, all five bodily senses come alive. Our body temperature, movements, balance, weight and vibrations - all get aligned with our senses in a symphonic way.

We are living in a situation where our nervous system is in constant stimulation and often our body and brain do not get an opportunity to calm down and relax. Due to this, our physical and mental conditions are often compromised. When we are stressed, catecholamines, a group of hormones made by our adrenal glands are released into the body to manage the stress. When catecholamines increase, our heart rate, blood pressure, breathing rate etc. will increase as a response to stress. But when we are in water, our body will alter the balance of catecholamines. Relaxation in the water can balance the catecholamines and help reduce our stress.

Biophilia & Water

Biophilia is the theory of love of life or living things. We have an intuitive and natural drive towards nature which is imprinted in our DNA. This deep-rooted connection with the natural world manifests in various forms. One of the most profound and essential elements that evoke our biophilic instincts is water. When we are near waterfalls, seashores, or rivers, the multisensory and immersive environment there positively influences our physiological and psychological states.

The rhythmic sound of water is commonly described as white noise. White noise contains all frequencies within the entire spectrum of sound in equal proportions. Because it has a broad range of sound bands, it is also known as broadband noise. White noise has a smoothening effect on the human brain. White noise serves as a masking agent for other distracting sounds and promotes relaxation. It will give a predictable and comforting environment that helps reduce stress and induce a state of calmness. Much research in this area demonstrates that white noise can improve work performance, mitigate the symptoms associated with ADHD (Attention-deficit Hyperactivity Disorder), and improve the quality of sleep.

Scientifically proven that the low frequency of the sound of water closely resembles the frequency of human breathing. Loud and disturbing noises are considered health hazards. People living in urban areas who are constantly exposed to loud and disturbing voices are often subjected to this threat. Introducing water sounds has been proven to be an effective solution for mitigating the problems associated with noise pollution. When we are introduced to a specific sound of water, it increases our relaxation state. It significantly contributes to easing stress.

Water biophilic design evolved in recent decades as a remedial for health and well-being. Biophilic design is an approach to architecture and interior design that seeks to incorporate and integrate elements of nature into built environments. Biophilic design enhances well-being, productivity, and overall experience by creating spaces that evoke a sense of connection with nature.

Along with natural lights, natural elements, natural materials and patterns, water features are one of the important aspects of biophilic design. Incorporating water elements, such as fountains, waterfalls, or indoor ponds, adds a dynamic and soothing component to the biophilic design. The sound and sight of flowing water contribute to a sense of tranquillity and connection with nature.

Hanging water-themed paintings, fountains or water-related showpieces in our homes or offices, can affect us psychologically. Seeing these elements daily has a profound impact on our brain and mind.

When we regularly witness a visual stimulation of an object or thing, a part of the brain responsible for seeing is activated. This visual cortex is primarily responsible for making choices and processing visual information. When we see an image or movement, the visual cortex will slowly stimulate our response and explain to the brain what we are witnessing. The more we see something, the more our brain gets used to it and starts connecting it with our thoughts and choices. This visual interpretation can slowly impact our choices similar to how frequent exposure to advertisements can influence our decisions. For children, this influence is more dominant. What they see around them plays a big role in what they like and choose. The presence of certain images or objects shapes their preferences 90% of the time.

Biophilic design spaces promote well-being, enhance productivity, and foster a deeper connection with nature through visual stimulations. It recognizes the profound impact that water has on our physical, mental, and emotional health. It will bring the benefits of the natural world into our everyday surroundings. Incorporating a biophilic water design in our living and working spaces will help us maintain our mental and emotional health and accelerate our efficiency in managing things.

Floating in Water

The density of the water and our body is similar. A 100-kg body will weigh only 5 kg in water, as most of our body consists of water and a certain percentage of air and fat which is lesser than the density of water. That's why we can float.

Buoyancy is the upward force applied on an object submerged in water. Buoyant force happens due to the difference in pressure between the top and bottom of the object. This force acts in the opposite direction to the force of gravity and allows objects to float. It is based on Archimedes' principles. He discovered this while he was in the bathtub.

The buoyancy effect is often given as a prescribed procedure by doctors to overcome stress and relax our minds and bodies. Swimming, floating, immersing or being in the water or any kind of water sport is highly beneficial. As the water pushes you to the top, it helps you in pushing the stress away as well. Being with water is an essential activity in ecotherapy and wilderness therapy for treating psychiatric, addiction, and trauma patients.

When we are in a homeostasis state, we function at optimal levels, both physically and mentally. But stress can disrupt this delicate balance, leading to the development of serious diseases. Floatation is used as a proven method for stress management. To comprehend this, we have to look into certain aspects of brain performance.

Our brain is an electrochemical organ, and a fully functioning brain can generate about 10 watts of electric power. This electrical activity of the brain is described as brainwaves, which fall into four categories - alpha, beta, theta, and delta.

When our brain is actively engaged in an activity, it generates beta waves. These waves signify a strongly engaged mind, comparable to low amplitude and high frequency ranging from 15 to 40 cycles per second. Whereas a calm and restful state induces the generation of alpha waves, indicating a relaxed mind with a reduced frequency between 9 to 14 cycles per second.

When we are in a mentally disengaged state, the brain enters theta wave mode, a more calming and relaxing state than alpha featuring a frequency of 4 to 8 cycles per second. Finally, when we are in deep sleep, or a state of deep meditation, the brainwaves reach their greatest amplitude and slowest frequently between 2 to 3 cycles per second referred to as the delta state. Many scientific studies underscore that when we enter a floatation or submerged state in water or with water for a reasonable amount of time, our brain showcases the pattern dominated by alpha and theta waves, indicating a calm, relaxed, and meditative state.

Restricted Environmental Stimulation Therapy (REST) is a floating experience in the water like being in a zero-gravity environment. During this therapy, individuals float on a bed of water saturated with Epsom salt. It is like the experiences in the Dead Sea. This floating experience is designed to remove sensory inputs like touch, gravity, light, sound etc. which allows our senses to calm and relax with water.

This kind of floatation in a controlled environment promotes our athletic performances, reduces anxiety and stress, relieves physical pain, and promotes good sleep. The REST flotation concept has been popular in the USA since the 1950s. Dr. Jay Shurley and Dr. John Lilly at the National Institute of Mental Health, USA discovered the therapeutic benefits of floating. A weekly or monthly float in the water has an overall effect on stress and anxiety reduction.

Immersing in Water

Our brain has two parts, called hemispheres and it is cross wired with the body. The left hemisphere controls the right part of the body, and the right hemisphere controls the left part of the body. The left brain functions as our analytical, speech, arithmetic, writing, and logical parts and the right part functions as our creative, skill, spatial, and artistic parts.

Our educational system and teaching method are mostly aligned with left-brain learning. From childhood, we tend to get used in left brain centric methodologies. We often overlook the aspects of right brain development. The balanced approach was often taken backstage in the earlier education system. However, nowadays, left and right brain teaching strategies are an important part of the education curriculum design. Many studies find that being in water regularly and activities like floating, swimming, water sports etc. can improve the functioning of the right hemisphere. This helps to amplify the optimal function of the creative, analytical, and artistic parts of our brain.

When we immerse ourselves in water, we undergo a profound experience of positive feelings. The duration and intensity of these emotions depend upon the circumstances and our internal state of mind. The more actively we engage with water, the fewer negative feelings we tend to experience. This is why water sports or water-based activities are considered not only recreational but also therapeutic.

Positive emotions fall into two categories: Hedonia and Eudaimonia. Hedonia is related to our senses and Eudaimonia is related to our overall well-being or doing good. According to research, 40% of our happiness and positive feelings can be derived from engaging in meaningful activities. Engaging in meaningful water-based activities can contribute to elevating our overall happiness index.

Brain and water

When we are with water, a group of neurons in our brain is activated. This stimulation will activate some neurological functions that impact our attention, cognition, grasping power, emotional responses, and certain brain processing capabilities. Our brain is a very complex, deep, and intelligent organ which is least understood. Its complexity is similar to the nature of water. When the two are together, a unique relationship unfolds.

The brain creates and changes its neurological networks constantly to accomplish its effectiveness based on various situations. Similarly, water undergoes constant structural changes in every millisecond to adapt to the situations.

Neuroscientists believe that our cerebral cortex is the seat of consciousness. When we see a full moon, the sight captured by our eyes undergoes processing in the retina stimulating the photoreceptors. This information then travels to the brain, where a visual image is processed. Later, these images linger in our visual consciousness for a long time and are forever linked with our minds and brains. This illusionary concept is part of our consciousness.

Similarly, water, with its dynamic dance of atoms due to hydrogen bonding, exhibits a conscious response, showcasing distinguish characteristics each time it encounters a new situation. This polarity of water is the basis of life and plays an important role in our daily functioning. The charge separation of oxygen and hydrogen provides a unique structure to the water. It is water's "internal intelligence". This inherent intelligence allows life ingredients to create a structure without any external directions or guidance.

Our brains are wired positively and negatively. However, the negative is more prominent to keep our survival instinct high. That's why negative experiences tend to get a stronger reaction from us. But regular exposure to water, whether in the form of rivers, lakes, or seas, can have a significant impact on the happiness pathways of our brain. Our engagement with water creates positive experiences which can strengthen the positive neural pathways. This positive impact will increase the levels of dopamine, endorphins, and serotonin.

Also, spending time with water can lower the level of stress-inducing hormones like norepinephrine, epinephrine, and cortisol. Neuroendocrinologists support the idea that water and brain chemistry share a significant relationship. The effective use of water can alter and influence the chemical and hormonal secretions in the brain, influencing moods, emotions, and responses. The powerful relationship between the hypothalamus and water is detailed in this book.

From ancient practises to modern science, both have a common understanding that we have three kinds of brains due to evolutionary processes: Reptile, Paleomammalian and Neocortex. In simple terms, we can refer to them as the reptile, mammal, and conscious brain.

The reptile brain emerges first during our womb stay. It controls our bodily functions and is fundamentally geared for our survival. The mammal brain governs our emotions, bonding, muscle memory, habits, and decisions. What sets us apart from other species is the development of the neocortex brain, responsible for higher mental functions, cognitive abilities, memory, consciousness, perspectives and various other functions.

Being with water regularly offers a remarkable benefit to all three brains. It promotes relaxation and alertness, supporting the reptile brain's control over bodily function. Also, water makes a harmonious interrelationship between body and mind by influencing the mammal brain. Similarly, water brings a dramatic improvement in the neocortex brain, aiding the effective management of cognitive functions, memory, and intellectual aspects. When we are with water, the neocortex brain becomes the most active part of the human brain.

Connect with Water

Having a bath in an open stream, river, pond, or sea is a luxury for most of us. However, whenever it's possible, dip into a water source near you. Spending time near the ocean, walking along the shoreline, and listening to the sound of waves can be incredibly soothing. If you have access to a river or lake, spending time there can be great practice.

Observe when we are with water. The sound and sight of flowing water can help reduce stress, lower anxiety levels, and promote a peaceful state of mind. Many people find that being near water can stimulate creativity and provide mental clarity. The rhythmic flow and sound of water can have a soothing effect. It allows our mind to relax, focus, and enhance creative thinking.

When you find a waterfall nearby, sit or stand close enough to feel the spray, and engage with it. Allow the sound and sight of the rushing water to calm your mind. Engaging in activities like swimming, snorkelling, or kayaking can provide a deeper connection with water. Whenever you're near a flowing stream, or lake, or taking a bath, you can practice mindfulness with water. Focus your attention on the sensation of water on your skin, the sound it makes, and the way it moves. Allow yourself to fully experience and appreciate the presence of water. Adopt a practice that our family vacations and picnics involve some activities near a natural water body.

Water's dynamic dance of atoms and its distinctive features and anomalies collectively contribute to an intelligence that plays a fundamental role in our existence. We must be in proximity to water and harness the benefits water offers us. Fall deeply in love with water and cultivate a profound connection with it. It will heal you, and make you better, stronger, and emotionally stable.

Where it All Begins & Ends...

"Water is life's matter and matrix, mother and medium. There is no life without water."

— Albert Szent-Gyorgyi

My first feeling about water was fear. When I was a child, every monsoon brought thunders, lightning, and heavy rains, making it a terrifying experience. Most of the time, the monsoon arrived on the school opening day after our summer vacations. The fear of storms continued during June and July, disrupting school as the rain would often continue for days. During those stormy nights, I would tightly embrace my mother, seeking comfort in her presence, and praying to every God I know. For our villagers who depend on agriculture, these months were named *"panjamasam"*, or dearth months, as prolonged rains disrupted agricultural activities.

My mother and aunt were both raised in the village of Aranmula, surrounded by paddy fields and water streams which eventually connected with the river Pampa. They too faced chaos of monsoons in their own lives. Their homes will be isolated for months as the paddy field submerged. However, over time, like many others in the village, they forged a connection with water. Learning to swim and row became an essential life skill for them. Slowly, they managed the challenges of the monsoon into an adventure. My mother and aunt become experienced swimmers and rowers. They found entertainment in catching small fish and engaging in water-based games, turning the once fearful months into opportunities for joy.

When they relocated from Aranmula to Vazhoor, the luxury of being surrounded by water was reduced, but their bond with water lived through storytelling and their childhood adventures. As their son, my dislike for water sometimes felt like an embarrassment.

One summer day, my mother and I visited a small lake near our house for bathing. While she was busy washing clothes, I hesitantly sat by the shore, putting my legs into the water, and observing the lazy movement of the fish. Suddenly, my mother gently pushed me into the water. Before I could react, water enveloped me, and I began to sink. Panic seized me as I struggled to resurface, but then, water cradled me and lifted me effortlessly to the surface. My mother, unfazed by my initial fear, lifted me out of the water and told me, "See, water won't let you drown because she is your mother too".

Her comment was beyond my understanding. She continued, "Come with me, I will show you something". She carried me into the water and started swimming. As I clung to her, my fears slowly started dissolving. That day, I witnessed the underwater world for the first time. I saw the fish, plants, roots of lotus flowers, fading sunlight and many other things. By the time we emerged, I was no longer afraid of water. My fear was replaced by a newfound love, and I wanted to be with water. I learned to swim, and from that day, heavy rains, thunderstorms, and lightning lost their impact on me.

In my adolescence, swimming across the rivers – Manimala, Pampa and Meenachil, became a favourite pastime for me and my friends. We spend our weekends renting cycles, making friendly bets, and challenging the currents of the rivers. Somehow these experiences are more enjoyable to us than any other activities. The rivers became our playground, a source of joy that persisted for years.

I have narrated my near-death illness in the preface of this book. During this time, while many doubted my chances of recovery, my mother and aunt were very confident about my survival. Doctors treated me with medicine, and my mother and aunt turned to prayers and the transformative power of water. They firmly believed in water's supernatural properties.

When I recovered and spent some time with them, I began to question their conviction. In response, they tried to convince me with stories from *Puranas* and *Upanishads*, sacred Hindu literature that serve as the encyclopaedias of Hinduism. These texts cover not only the mythological tales of gods but also explore cosmology, geology, genealogy, theology, philosophy, astronomy, mineralogy, medicine, love, karma, dharma, and various other aspects of life. These are the influential literature of Hinduism and are known for the symbolism portrayed in the stories. I feel one such story I heard from my mother will be appropriate to conclude this book.

Samudra Mathanam or Churning of the ocean is a vividly depicted event in Hindu scriptures. This narrative, involving both devas and asuras gives symbolic aspects of the relationship of water with our body and mind. *Samudra mathanam* has profound meanings and symbolism in the aspects of the universe. Its artistical expressions can be seen in India's parliament building, Bangkok's Suvarnabhumi International Airport, Cambodia's Angkor Wat, and various other places.

Devas and Asuras are half-brothers, but both are in constant fights with each other. Devas live in *Devaloka*, a place above the sky that is often referred to as paradise and Asuras live in *Patala*, a place beneath the ocean. Most of the time the earth is the warzone for their conflict.

The narrative takes a pivotal turn when Lord Indra, king of Devas is cursed by sage *Durvasa*. Due to this curse, the devas lost immortality, strength, and fortune. Seizing this opportunity, Asuras defeated Devas in a war, and they gained control of the *Devaloka* and the universe.

Facing this dire situation, the devas, in a quest to regain their immortality and fortune, approached God Vishnu for counsel. Acting on his advice, an alliance formed between the devas and asuras. Their common objective is to get *Amrut*, the nectar of immortality. Both parties jointly decided to churn the Milky Ocean to obtain the *Amrut* and share it equally. They started churning the ocean using Mount Meru as a churning rod and serpent king *Vasuki* as a churning rope.

As the cosmic churning unfolds, numerous things emerge from the depths of the milky ocean. Finally, *Dhanvathari*, the heavenly physician appeared from the ocean with a pot containing *Amrut*, the nectar of immortality.

This tale will take a different turn from here. Devas did not share the *Amrut* with Asuras. They tricked Asuras with the help of Lord Vishnu and consumed the *Amrut*. From there onwards, this deceitful act sets the stage for an eternal cycle of warfare between devas and asuras.

Beyond this literal narrative, this holds many important symbolic significances. However, I want to limit the scope of this tale to explain the symbolic meaning of the churning process to relate the relationship of water with us.

Mythological aspects have various meanings. It narrates the symbolic, scientific, cultural, logical, and religious aspects often with moral and ethical qualities. Devas and Asuras symbolize the positive and negative aspects of human personality. Their ceaseless conflicts mirror the universal struggle between good and evil. Their collaboration in the ocean-churning process represents the unity of positive and negative thoughts. The churning process represents the eternal struggle between positive and negative forces in the universe, also in our minds.

The choice of water for the medium of this churning holds a profound significance. Water encapsulates both positivity and negativity without any discrimination. Water embodies different qualities and archetypes and plays specific roles in the cosmic drama, illustrating various aspects of the cosmic order.

Water represents many aspects and holds multiple symbolic meanings. The Milky Ocean represents the Milky Way, the source of life created in the universe, and existence itself. Also, water is extraterrestrial. It symbolizes the vast and infinite potential from which every life arises. The churning of the ocean purifies the waters, removing impurities. This process can be seen as an allegory for the purification and transformation of an individual's mind and consciousness.

During the churning, various objects and beings emerged from the ocean. This emergence of diverse objects and things signifies the continuous cycle of creation, sustenance and dissolution based on a cosmic order. It is narrated that 14 different things emerged from water during the churning process.

The first thing that emerged was Lakshmi, the goddess of wealth and fortune symbolizing our physical and mental well-being states of us. Water balances physical and psychological well-being.

Secondly, the four *Apsaras* emerged. *Apa* means water and *Saras* means energy and *Apsaras* means the energy of water. *Apsaras* as described as nymphs and the female spirit of water, symbolize love, sexuality, pleasure, and compassion. As per yogic meditation, the *swathishtana chakra* or the water chakra is associated with sensuality, creativity, flexibility, energy, control, emotions, feelings, and nourishment. Water is controlling and actively participating in these major functions of us.

Subsequent things that emerged from the water also symbolize human aspirations, addictions, expressions, and various other aspects. *Sura*, who appeared during the churning process is considered the creator of alcohol and represents our psychic limitations and additions. Three types of supernatural animals appeared from the water, *Kamdhenu*, a wish-granting cow, *Airavata*, the white elephant and *Uchhaishravas*, a seven-headed horse. These creatures symbolise human aspirations.

Similarly, three valuable possessions emerged. *Koustuba*, the most valuable jewel, *Parijat*, is a divine flowering tree and a powerful bow. Apart from this, other things that emerged from *Samudra Manthan* are the Moon, *Jyeshta*, the goddess of misfortune, *Tulsi* the plant, *Shankha*, the conch, and *Nidra* the slot. These emergencies are the representation of human aspiration to achieve impossible connotations. Each represents the humans' tendency to earn and possess various supernatural abilities and the consequences of the same.

The search for immortality itself can be considered a metaphor for higher knowledge and divine realization. Finally, the physician, *Dhanvantari*, represents the overall health and well-being and the *Amrut*, the nectar of immortality.

Amrut is repeatedly referred to as the drink of gods like *ambrosia* in Greek mythology. In yogic philosophy, *Amrut* is described as the sublime flow of water flowing from the pituitary gland to the back of the throat when a certain level of deep meditation is achieved. It does not mean necessarily the absence of death or the elixir of life. From a philosophical point, *Amrut* represents an elevated state of self-awareness and a supreme level of self-realisation. Water plays that role beautifully.

Nature has always maintained a proper balance of the five basic elements. Earth or land, Sun or Light, Water, Air, and Ether. Any disturbance of this natural balance creates troubles for every living creature and even for the universe. From the very beginning, our ancestors understood these fundamental principles and they formed a natural relationship with nature. They knew that any action, movement, creation, change and destruction are the result of the forces beyond their control and hence recognized divinity in nature. Water enjoyed that divinity.

Water has long been a symbol in art, movies, and poetry, representing various emotions and themes. Movies and poems show calm lakes, gentle streams, or calm ocean waves to evoke a sense of tranquillity. Rain or stormy seas symbolize grief, heartbreak, or a sense of loss in emotional scenes. The image of rain or a flowing river can signify the cleansing of the past and the opportunity for a fresh start. The crashing waves, turbulent storms, or powerful waterfalls can be used to show dramatic or intense emotions such as anger, passion, or determination. The imagery of vast oceans or open seas evokes a sense of liberation, escape, and exploration. Dark, deep waters or foggy rivers can be used to create an atmosphere of mystery, unknown possibilities, or hidden depths of emotions. Mirroring surfaces like still lakes or calm ponds represent the process of self-discovery, reflection, and introspection.

This list of situations with artistic and creative expressions with water can go on and on. I don't think any other thing in the world has such wide imagery to convey unique emotions or meanings other than water.

The oceans served as the cradle for the first microorganisms, providing a nurturing environment for the formation of complex organic molecules and the evolution of life. From the depths of ancient seas, life gradually emerged, marking the beginning of a remarkable journey. As life unfolds, water remains a constant companion, weaving its way through the tapestry of existence.

As life reaches its inevitable end, water assumes a different role—a symbol of departure and transition. The absence of water marks the finality of life. In many cultures, water is associated with purification, renewal, and the transition to the afterlife. It is used in rituals and ceremonies to bid farewell, to cleanse, and to symbolize the journey into the unknown.

With all these facts and profound meanings and information found in all religious, social, and scientific literature telling us for centuries and narrowing down to one single aspect - take care of water so that it takes care of you. Handle water with respect, it will give a thousand-fold back to you. Sit with water and it will help you meditate. Play with it, it will heal you, cherish you and make you a better individual in all aspects. What else do we need?

Throughout history, water has played a pivotal role in shaping the rise and fall of civilizations. While water is essential for sustenance and growth, it can also be a destructive force capable of ruining the mightiest of civilizations. Harappan civilization, one of the earliest urban civilizations in the world, has been impacted by shifts in the course of rivers, leading to water scarcity and ecological disruption. The changing patterns of water flow led to an array of events, and the ultimate downfall of this once-thriving civilization. The inability to effectively manage water resources contributed to the decline and eventual abandonment of several ancient Mesopotamian cities. A prolonged period of drought is believed to have severely impacted the Maya civilization. The lack of water availability, combined with societal and political challenges, led to the decline of the Khmer civilization.

These examples demonstrate how water has historically played a significant role in the decline and eventual destruction of ancient societies. Whether through devastating floods, prolonged droughts, contaminated or polluted water, or mismanagement of resources, water's destructive power has proven capable of toppling once-thriving civilizations. These historical lessons teach us the importance of responsible water management which adapts to changing environmental conditions in our times.

Giving back to water is not only an act of gratitude but also a responsibility we have towards the environment and future generations. Remember, every action, no matter how small, can make a difference.

Every life begins and ends with water — this profound statement encapsulates the vital role that water plays in the cycle of life.

Acknowledgements

Writing a book about water was never on my agenda. In fact, penning down a book seemed like a distant possibility. My heartfelt gratitude goes to those who supported, encouraged and insisted on the realisation of this endeavour.

It all started in 2015 when I commenced "Water - Ideas for Life" program, a condensed presentation and talk show summarizing the content of this book. Following each program, the curious and enthusiastic queries from attendees played a key role in prompting me to imagine the idea of publishing this book. I express my sincere thanks to all those whose curiosity and engagement laid the foundation for this book.

I owe my journey into the words of books to Mr Ramachandran Nair, my schoolmate Parthasarathy's father. He persistently and influentially nurtured my reading habit from an early age. His support and the ample books he provided became the foundation of the bibliophile me.

I was an average student and never had any aspirations in education. However, the saying, "It is the teachers that make the difference, not the classroom", held true in my life. I am grateful to my schoolteachers especially, Ammukkutty Amma, Madhusudhana Kaimal, Lalithambika, and Sarojini teacher, all of whom played an important role in nurturing my education. Their constant love and guidance were the reason for my academic survival.

I am very much obligated to my childhood friends who stood by me through thick and thin, supporting and encouraging my budding skills. My thanks go to Jijith Kumar P, Sinu Lal K, Ranjith Kumar, Biju Kutty K B, and Mohan Vazhoor. I extend my sincere thanks to my friends at our theatre troupe, Deepti Handwritten magazine, IPTA, and the clubs I was associated with in my growing years.

Fate led me to the water treatment industry where I crossed paths with Mr Jeco John. His introduction opened the door to the world of industrial water treatment, and I am grateful for the opportunity to work under his guidance during the initial years of my career. Additionally, I owe much to the late Mr Sameer Nerurkar, my first mentor in the physical, chemical, and biological aspects of water treatment. His recognition of my interest in the subject coupled with his provision of books, and insights into water laid the foundation of my career.

The trajectory of my career owes much to the guidance of Major H.L. Khajuria, who entrusted me with responsibility and provided a free hand in shaping my path as a water treatment professional. Our enduring association for over five years played a pivotal role in shaping my professional journey.

I am indebted to Mr. Madhan Gopal S., my colleague and friend, with whom I shared four years of travel and stay across various locations in India. Our open-minded discussions during these travels contributed to shaping my curiosity about the mysteries of water.

My sincere thanks go out to my colleagues in Gea Energy Systems Limited (Now BGR Energy Systems Limited), especially, Murasu K Senthil, M.S. Prthvi, V. Ganesh, A. Varada Chari, K. Prabhakar, T.K Padmanabhan, Donald Rose, Anbazhagan, Veera Raghavan, Stanley Christopher, Anand, Sasi Kumar, Swadhin Samantaray, Hitesh Hemani, Ganapathi Raman, T. Ganesh, Loganathan, D. Siva Kumar, S. Visagan, Joydeep Mukherji, R. Rajaram, Amutha Devi, J. H. Naidu, Madhusoodanan, G A Prakash, Balakrishnan, Chezhian, and Magesh Babu for their valuable contributions and support to shape my journey in the water sector.

I extend my thanks to the entire team of Ambika Projects and DSPL where I progressed through my journey as an entrepreneur. Their questions and discussion on various chapters of water enriched the content of this book. Special appreciation goes to Mr. Deena Dhayalan for his involvement and encouragement in developing this book.

Water – Ideas for Life (WIL) program generated numerous discussions, and I extend my gratitude to everyone who attended and assisted in organising the program – clients, colleagues, associates and friends alike. Your enquiries and ideas propelled me to embrace my role as a writer.

My deepest thanks are reserved for Mr Sudhir Gupta, Sohail Gupta, Sanjay Gupta and their families for their continuous support and encouragement. I also express my sincere gratitude to the Gupta Group of companies for their persistent support throughout this undertaking.

Editing this book presented a formidable challenge, and I am thankful to Ms Kavya Sadashivan for the preliminary editing of the book and Mr Amit Vasudev for the final editing. I am very thankful for their commitment and energy in refining its content and their efforts have significantly contributed to the quality of this book.

The illustrations and drawings contributed significantly to understanding certain concepts and simplification of ideas presented in this book. All drawings are created by Arjun Nair, the artist, and the Illustrations are shaped by Mr. Dhanush. Both showed a good understanding of the concept and a degree of creativity. I extend my gratitude to both for their imagination and exceptional effort in enhancing the reading experiences.

In the journey of writing this book, the contribution of inquisitive minds has illuminated the path with fresh perspectives. I extend my gratitude to Santhosh Prasad, Vikram Nataraj and my son, Harsh Vardhan for exemplifying such curiosity that weaved the final fabric of this book.

Finally, the realisation of this book would not have been possible without the intervention, corrections and advice from my wife Ambica Suresh. Her inspiration and support transformed my vague ideas into a book.

My heartfelt thanks to all who contributed in multiple ways to enhance the content presented in this book. I deeply admire the scientists, technologists, teachers, professionals, and writers who shared their research, stories, teachings, and insights. I genuinely respect your contributions and dedication. I also seek forgiveness for any errors that may exist in this book. Any mistakes in this book are mine alone.

References

1. Divine, Panacean and Emancipative Water in Vedic Religion- Rohana Seneviratne

2. A short history of nearly everything – Bill Bryson

3. The Water Kingdom- Philip Ball

4. The fourth phase of water – Dr Gerlad Pollack

5. Water cure manual by Joel Shew M.D.

6. The beginning of life by Isaac Asimov

7. Some aspects of Ecology from Vedas – M.M. Trigunayat

8. Life of Vincent Priessnitz- Founder of Hydropathy by Richard Metcalfe

9. Hydropathy- The cold water cure – Vincent Priessnitz

10. Revival of Swedish Vedic and traditional wisdom of water management – An effective tool to mitigate water crisis – D.D. Ozha & V.N. Mathur

11. Islam and water – Laura Wickstrom

12. Effect of storage of water in different metal vessels on coliforms- Sreedevi Sarsan

13. The Quran and modern science - Dr Maurice Bucaille

14. Your body, Many cries of water - F. Batmanghelidj, M.D.

15. The Tao of Water - Rod Giblet

16. Ayurvedic references in Adharva Veda - Dr. Ch. Sivaramakrishna Sarma M.A., M.A., Ph.D.

17. Origin of environmental science from Vedas – Shashi Tiwari

18. Water – Key driving force – P.S. Datta

19. The concept of water in Rig Veda – Dr Chandini Saxena

20. Water in the Bible – Earthcare forum

21. Water as a common reference for monastic lives and spaces in Cistercian and Han Buddhist monasteries- Weiqiao Wang & Jiang Feng

22. The water therapy manual by Vance Ferrell

23. Guidelines of drinking water quality – Fourth edition WHO

24. Sacredness of water in Hindu tradition – Dr Kala Acharya

25. Water for Health: An overview of principles & practices of Water consumption in Ayurveda- Deepak Londhe, Chuliveri Ashwin Chandra, Uday Ravi Sekhar Namburi, Shobhit Kumar, Shital Chinchalkar, Sudha Kumari Chuliveri

26. The water wizard- Extraordinary properties of natural water by Viktor Schauberger.

27. Floatation therapy for specific health concerns by Laura Witte, PhD, PA-C, Carlos Santo, ND, Mark E. Archambault, DHSc, PA-C, DFAAPA, Thomas Colletti, DHSc, PA-C, DFAAPA, and Randy Danielsen, PhD, PA-C Emeritus, DFAAPA.

28. Water immersion and flotation: From stress experiment to stress treatment by Peter Suedfeld, Elizabeth J. Ballard, Margaux Murphy

29. The water cure applied to every known disease by J.H. Rausse & C.H. Meeker

30. Origin of environmental sciences from Vedas by Sashi Tiwari

31. Jacques Benveniste by Geoff watts

32. The memory of water: Homeopathy and the battle of ideas in the new science by Michel Schiff

33. Ghosts of molecules: The case of memory of water by Francis Beauvais

34. The water Book by Alok Jha.

35. Water – A short introduction by John Finney

36. An autobiography of water by Philip ball

37. The Hidden messages of water by Dr. Musaru Emoto

38. Experiencing with water by Robert Gardner

39. The True power of water by Dr Musaru Emoto

40. Universal Water by Dr West Marrin

41. Water – The life-supporting resource by Robert Gardner

42. The spirit molecule- A doctor's revolutionary research into the biology of near- death and mystical experiences By Rick Strassman MD

43. Biological effect of magnetic water on humans and animals – Biomedical science 2017, By Azab Elsayed Azab.

44. **Pilot Aquaphotomic Study of the Effects of Audible Sound on Water Molecular Structure by Stefano Materazzi.**

45. Effects of nature sounds on the attention and physiological and psychological relaxation by Injoon Song, Kwangsik Baek, Choyun Kim, and Chorong Song

46. Significance of Water from a Buddhist Perspective By Wimal Hewamanage

47. Origin of Water Ice in the Solar System by Jonathan I. Lunine

48. Water: The Science of Nature's Most Important Nutrient by Len Kravitz, Ph.D.

49. The Chemistry of Water Professor Jill Granger

50. The many mysteries of water by David Robson and Michael Marshall

51. The World in a Drop: Memory and Forms of Thought in Water by Dr. Bernd Kroplin

52. The oxford handbook of Atheism by Juhem Navarro – Rivera and Ariela Keysar

53. Vedas (Rig, Yagur, Sama & Atharva), Bhagwat Gita, Mahabharata, The Bible, The Quran, Tao Te Ching, Book of Amos, Book of Isaiah, Various Puranas and Upanishads, Gruha suktam, Agamas, Various Hadiths. (Referred to many of these scriptures/ books published in Malayalam, Hindi, Sanskrit and English)

54. Various journals and articles published in Nature – Scientific reports.

55. Various reports published by the American Association for the Advancement of Science (AAAS), Science Direct and Royal Society.